RESTORED TO GLORY

RESTORED TO GLORY

A GUIDE TO RENOVATING YOUR PERIOD HOME

Charlie Luxton & Sally Bevan

BBC
BOOKS

This book is published to accompany the television series *Restored to Glory*, made for BBC2 by BBC Format Entertainment
Series Producer: Amy Joyce
Executive Producer: Martin Scott
Creative Head of Format Entertainment: Richard Hopkins

First published 2005

ISBN 0 563 49350 X

Published by BBC Books, BBC Worldwide Limited, Woodlands, 80 Wood Lane, London W12 0TT

This edition produced for The Book People Ltd, Hall Wood Avenue, Haydock, St Helens WA11 9UL

Commissioning editor: Vivien Bowler
Project editor: Martin Redfern
Designer: Isobel Gillan
Picture researcher: Victoria Hall
Production controller: Kenneth McKay

Printed and bound in Italy by L.E.G.O. SpA
Colour separations by Butler and Tanner Origination

AUTHORS' ACKNOWLEDGEMENTS

Huge thanks to everyone who worked on *Restored to Glory* and helped make it such fun. I would especially like to thank the home-owners, whose vision and enthusiasm for their properties made the series possible. They were all incredibly hospitable to us during filming, and welcomed us into the precious comfort of their cosy corners and caravans during some very cold, very long days on site. Tea was never in short supply and neither was good humour. I hope their example inspires more people to tackle restoration and achieve their dream.

Charlie Luxton

Many thanks to everyone at BBC Books, especially Viv and Martin who are always such a pleasure to work with. Huge gratitude and love also go to those who helped me research and write the book, especially Jan and Andrew, Ben and Lisa, and Al. This book is for Maddy, the newest addition to the clan.

Sally Bevan

PRODUCERS' ACKNOWLEDGEMENTS

BBC Format Entertainment would like to thank Fenia Vardanis, Jane Lush and Roly Keating at the BBC. They would also like to thank Martin Morrison, Kate Scholefield, Sue Hills, Tina Bolton-Stott and the whole production team for all their hard work.

CONTENTS

FOREWORD by Charlie Luxton

A good restoration is a thing to stir the soul. At a time when appearance is king, when it doesn't seem to matter how well something works as long as it looks good, the fact that people pour love and effort into rejuvenating old buildings warms my heart. It is the antithesis of surface beauty because so much of the blood, sweat, tears and hard cash that go into restoring an old building are never seen. Quick fixes, like a lick of paint or wallpaper, produce an instant 'refreshed' look. The hours spent chipping out and repointing a wall can simply leave you with something looking pretty much just as it did when you started. I reckon that about two-thirds of restoration is unseen, but the finished product has an integrity you can't surpass. Handcrafted, natural materials that are painstakingly worked exude a quality that makes quick-fix surface treatments look exactly what they are. It is true that the lengths some people go to can seem obsessive, but the satisfaction gained from doing a job properly is very hard to beat, and the harder, dirtier and longer the job, the more rewarding it is.

Time and again the *Restored to Glory* TV series shows the superiority of good over fast, not least in Middi's immaculate restoration of Tan Farm Cottages, a beautiful 500-year-old timber-frame house in Essex. He spent hundreds of hours and thousands of pounds meticulously replacing half the timbers, each one carefully shaped and pegged into place, to create a masterpiece. Then, in order to protect his hard work, he covered most of them up with plaster, leaving just a few visible on the inside. His hard work will never be seen from the outside, but Middi knows he has revitalized and protected the house so that it will stand for another 500 years.

ABOVE LEFT Weeks of patient work were required at Heolas Fawr in Wales to make good the stone walls.

RIGHT The ruins at Biddulph, Staffordshire, are all that is left of the grand house that was destroyed by cannon in the Civil War. An amazing piece of living history.

Beneath the bland concrete render of Tan Farm Cottages in Essex lay a fifteenth-century timber-frame house.

Les and Dee at Par Bridge Crossing Cottage in Cornwall did a similar thing with their chimneys. They took down their only remaining one to see how it was built, then rebuilt it and the two missing chimneys in the correct fashion. However, having rebuilt the first one with a reclaimed local brick, they decided that the colour and size looked wrong, so they took it down and rebuilt it again. The result is three new chimneys built five times that look like they've always been there. While nobody would know the heartache that has gone into

PROPERTY **Tan Farm Cottages, Essex**
BUILT **Early to mid-fifteenth century**
CURRENT OWNERS **Middi and Susan De Luca**
PURCHASE PRICE **£200,000**
RESTORATION BUDGET **£30,000**
RESTORATION SCHEDULE **10 months**

Tan Farm Cottages were in a terrible condition when Middi and Susan bought them at auction a couple of years ago. The auctioneers failed to see the age of the building beneath a thick skin of cement render but Middi spotted the fifteenth-century jetted timber-framed house through the grime and decay. However even he didn't realize the terrible state the frame was in: the cement render was in fact holding it together. Middi has painstakingly dismantled and repaired the entire building himself. He is a self-taught restorer with a real love of timber. Both the house and the way it has been restored really impressed our experts.

PROPERTY **Biddulph Old Hall, Staffordshire**
BUILT **1580. Rebuilt 1650, with later additions in the nineteenth century**
CURRENT OWNERS **Nigel Daly and Brian Vowels**
PURCHASE PRICE **£537,000**
RESTORATION BUDGET **£500,000**
RESTORATION SCHEDULE **10 months**

This early sixteenth-century hall house was extended with a large Flemish-inspired courtyard in the late sixteenth century. The extension was destroyed during the Civil War, and, having fallen on hard times, the owners moved back into the original hall, which they extended again in the late seventeenth century. Additions were made in 1820 to create a large rambling property. Prior to Nigel and Brian's purchase, the hall had fallen into such a poor state of repair that its previous occupant had resorted to living in just a few of its many rooms.

restoring them, the satisfaction Les and Dee got from doing the job properly has made up for the effort.

It takes a special kind of person to take on a restoration project. Seeing the magic and potential of a house through layers of decay, dirt or chintz takes real vision. Keeping that dream through the setbacks when you could easily opt for a stress-free alternative takes dedication. Over the past year and a half, while following the ins and outs of the series' seven projects, I've witnessed our contributors endure both backbreaking work and hardship that would have driven many people to despair. Take Brian and Nigel in Biddulph, Staffordshire, who throughout the winter and at all hours had to bail freezing water out of a stone trough whenever it rained in order to stop their cellar flooding. Or take Val and Les at Higher Hill Farm, who at the start of their project had two flights of stairs – one of stone, the other of wood. During the build the wooden one was removed so that a new concrete floor could be laid. Unfortunately, they forgot that they wouldn't be able to get to the stone staircase while the concrete set, so for two days the only way to get to their solitary bathroom was to cross the farmyard, go up a 3-metre (15-ft) ladder and climb in through the bathroom window. Not a pleasant experience, especially in the middle of the night. Les decided not to tell Val about this ... until late one night when she needed the loo. And I'll always have special memories of working with Gervase in Wales: we had to spread half a tonne of cow dung on the inside of his house's huge Welsh chimney to neutralize the soot acidity – an unforgettable experience, especially with the director shouting encouragement from a safe distance.

PROPERTY **Higher Hill Farm, Lancashire**
BUILT **Early seventeenth century**
CURRENT OWNERS **Les and Val Thomas**
PURCHASE PRICE **£520,000**
RESTORATION BUDGET **£150,000**
RESTORATION SCHEDULE **9 months**

A highly original Jacobean farmhouse, located on the moors near Preston, this beautiful stone house is the first restoration project undertaken by owners Val and Les. Formerly the property of the water board, it had been run down over the previous twenty years. Complete with garderobe (old-fashioned toilet), beautiful king post trusses in the roof and king mullion window this Grade II* property has had few later additions. It is an absolute treasure.

The solid, stout walls of Higher Hill Farm in Lancashire tell of its exposed and wind-swept location. Building and landscape in harmony.

In the UK we have a unique heritage of old houses, an asset that's been appreciated and protected for hundreds of years. But as the BBC series *Restoration* showed, hundreds of wonderful buildings are derelict, at risk of falling down, or in danger of being ruined by insensitive renovation and alterations. At the end of the day protecting and caring for this heritage often comes down to the individuals who own the buildings. The cynic might point out that the owners of a listed or historic house have a vested interest in protecting their asset. However my experience of people who tackle restoration is that they're prepared to go the extra mile. In every project we followed, each of our contributors poured love, work and money into their property that will not necessarily be reflected in its monetary value. Nigel and Brian in Biddulph have opened up every concealed window or door, even when it meant redesigning a carefully worked-out staircase. Les and Dee in Cornwall actually made their house smaller to get back the original proportions, even though it meant losing a quarter of their already small floor area. If our contributors are anything to go by, the country's heritage is in good hands.

Throughout the making of the TV series I've been constantly amazed at the interest shown in historic buildings by people from all walks of life. Everywhere we've been just about everyone has expressed a sincere appreciation for historic architecture: carpenters, electricians, estate agents, auctioneers, passers-by ... they all seem to love old houses. I hope that through this book and the TV series we have managed to provide people with a bit more background to this fascinating subject. A big part of the joy I get from architecture is knowing about its history because

PROPERTY **Heolas Fawr, Cardiganshire, Wales**
BUILT **Rebuilt in 1851 but the origins could date back to the 1700s**
CURRENT OWNERS **Gervase and Mary Jane Webb**
PURCHASE PRICE **£21,000**
RESTORATION BUDGET **£50,000**
RESTORATION SCHEDULE **8 months**

Heolas Fawr is thought to have been a Welsh long house, which was extended in the nineteenth century. The slate farmhouse is just a few miles from the sea in the far west of Cardiganshire. Its rural position appealed to Gervase and Mary Jane, who spent months stripping out the house, removing up to ten layers of carpet. Now they're painstakingly re-plastering and repointing the whole property using traditional methods. The family is also raising lambs and growing food to create their own version of *The Good Life*.

buildings are the result of a centuries-long interplay between ideas, needs, money and politics. Understanding how these forces have interacted is like following a conversation about our history and gives a fascinating insight into what shaped our country. Learning about the great cathedrals, castles and civic buildings shows one side of this story; delving into domestic architecture reveals the other. It tells us so much about everyday life from the past, revealing how you or I might have lived if born in a previous age.

But old houses are not just about looking back: they have so much to teach us today because they are a master class in ingenious, functional and beautiful design – from the simple cruck house to the elegant proportions of the Georgian terrace and the easy comfort of an Arts and Crafts design. The wisdom and beauty encapsulated in old buildings is making more and more people question the nature of 'progress'. As environmental issues become ever more pressing, old construction techniques and sustainable materials, such as timber framing, lime renders and mud, are finding their way back into general use again.

Finally, I want to offer a few words of advice to anyone thinking of tackling a restoration. Having witnessed most of our contributors' trials and tribulations, I think the main lesson to take away from their experiences is the importance of realism. Right from the beginning it's essential to be realistic about what you can achieve. None of our projects ran completely smoothly, and every one of them either took longer or cost more than anticipated – usually both! The nature of working on an old building means that you never quite know what you are up against until

Heolas Fawr, Wales, needed hundreds of hours of work and tonnes of lime to bring it back to a good condition.

you get started and pull away bits of panelling and lift up those old carpets. Unexpected discoveries make it very hard to keep to a timetable and in control of your budget. A project can quickly become very unenjoyable and stressful if you are up against impossible deadlines with little money. Be generous with your estimates and give yourselves lots of slack and a good contingency fund.

PROPERTY **Bedford House, Clackmannanshire, Scotland**
BUILT **1850, with later additions in the 1870s and 1950s**
CURRENT OWNERS **Mike and Mandy Watson**
PURCHASE PRICE **£95,000**
RESTORATION BUDGET **£100–150,000**
RESTORATION SCHEDULE **12 months**

Built in 1858 by a wealthy brewery family and located about an hour's drive north of Edinburgh, the house is a large Italianate-style Victorian villa. The original design was compromised first by a Victorian extension in the 1870s and again in the 1950s with an ugly new office wing. Its last occupants, the local council, used the building as offices for many years, sub-dividing rooms and covering up all the period details. Mike and Mandy bought the property very cheaply and hoped to achieve significant improvements on a very limited budget. Despite careful financial control and attempting a significant amount of work themselves, they have struggled to get the budget to match the sheer size of the property.

Par Bridge Crossing Cottage in Cornwall showed that you don't need a 400-year-old mansion to get a kick out of restoration.

Being well prepared with a properly planned and drawn-up project before you get started will help enormously. This is not to say you have to get an architect or designer involved. Just doing a simple plan and a schedule of works (a list of every single job that will need doing) gets information out of your head and on to paper, which is invaluable for all concerned. The secret of organizing a good build is getting the right

PROPERTY Grafham House, Surrey
BUILT 1863
CURRENT OWNER Dr Barbara Salvage
PURCHASE PRICE £900,000
RESTORATION BUDGET £500,000
RESTORATION SCHEDULE 7 months

This mid-nineteenth-century Gothic Revival rectory, designed by the architect Henry Woodyer, was in a terrible condition when Barbara bought it. The roof had gone and many of the windows, despite being boarded up, had been smashed by vandals. On our first visit the cameraman went through a rotten staircase. But under the dirt and decay was a lovely, well-made home with some beautiful Victorian wall paintings and fireplaces. The house has had a couple of ugly 1960s extensions that have been remodelled to complement the original design. The garden is being revitalized by mixing the original plantings with new ones. The project is huge and is being undertaken by a large professional team overseen by an architect.

PROPERTY **Par Bridge Crossing Cottage, Cornwall**
BUILT **1874**
CURRENT OWNERS **Leslie Cornell and Dee Wadham**
PURCHASE PRICE **£118,000**
RESTORATION BUDGET **£20,000**
RESTORATION SCHEDULE **10 months**

This level-crossing-keeper's cottage was built in 1873 by the Cornish Mineral Railways. The small, two-bedroom property was in a bad state of repair when Les and Dee bought it, but its connection to the railways and need for restoration made it an ideal project for them. Their restoration included opening up original windows, dismantling and rebuilding chimneystacks, removing an unsightly later bathroom extension and turning it into a one-bedroom home. Les and Dee have worked hard to create an idealized version of a bygone age.

jobs to happen seamlessly in the right order. If you can do that, which is far from easy, your project has a good chance of running smoothly. Drawing up plans and schedules helps predict what is going to happen where and when; it should also ensure that you make fewer costly mistakes. Whether you seek help to get this planning right is a difficult decision to make. A lot of people feel that the fees paid to an architect or project manager could be saved and used elsewhere on the project, but both Val and Les in Lancashire and Mike and Mandy in Scotland started without proper professional advice, which led to big delays and in both cases extended the projects by nearly a year. When you're living in a caravan you really have to question whether the short-term saving on fees is worthwhile, especially when it can lead to costly mistakes in the long term.

Although I've witnessed highs and lows throughout the series, I can honestly say that my interest in restoration has never been greater – in fact, it's grown into an obsession. I never bore of chatting about lime or discussing paint and render removal techniques. My wife has lots of fun teasing me about my expanding collection of exciting books on topics such as wooden joints, thatching and cob repair techniques. We're embarking on our first joint project to restore a thatched cottage; little does she realize that she'll soon be just as obsessive as me because restoration is totally absorbing and addictive. You have been warned!

70
70

SO YOU WANT TO RESTORE A HOUSE?

If you're one of the millions who've been tuning into BBC2's *Restored to Glory,* you're probably already fascinated by old buildings. You may be thinking of tackling a restoration project yourself, or you might just be curious to find out what's involved. Whatever the reason, it's fantastic to know that more and more people are passionate about period properties and want to repair, conserve or restore them to their former glory.

In fact, restoration has never been so popular. The success of the BBC's recent *Restoration* series highlighted just how much people care about Britain's built heritage. The programmes revealed not only that two-thirds of people prefer old buildings to new ones and would love to live in a period home, but that nine out of ten people are fired up by restoration issues.

So, this book is a gentle introduction to the subject of restoring your own property, aiming to whet your appetite and give you a solid grounding in some of the basic techniques you'll require. It's designed to fill the void between stylish coffee-table books on architecture and highly technical DIY manuals, neither of which are very practical for the first-time restorer. In this guide you'll find stacks of useful information about the different building materials available, along with historic snippets and suggestions for authentic period details. You'll also find lots of hints and tips to help you avoid common pitfalls and get the most from your period property.

The book is divided into three distinct parts. Part One takes a general look at some of the issues involved in taking on a restoration project – such as raising the necessary finances, finding a reliable builder and the responsibilities of owning a listed property. Part Two contains detailed practical guidance for using traditional building materials and techniques,

Before, *left*, and after, *above right*: restoration doesn't have to be about ancient buildings. Twentieth-century projects, such as this 1920s suburban house, can be just as rewarding.

including lime, timber, stone, glass, brick and metal. Part Three concentrates on the two areas that are often an afterthought for many house restorers: interior decoration and getting the garden into shape. And last, but by no means least, you'll find details of further reading and useful addresses, to enable you to start researching your own project and find people who can help you realize your dream.

Restoration projects come in many different guises, from a run-down farm, *above*, to a derelict Victorian villa, *right*. What hidden gems are lurking in your neighbourhood?

ARE YOU MAD TO TAKE IT ON?

Well, no actually. As our on-screen heroic house restorers will tell you, the joys of restoration are numerous and varied, far outweighing any setbacks you're bound to experience along the way. Restorers who take on a project often have lots of different motives for saving a crumbling property, which can include one or more of the following.

Historical interest

Living in a historic building is a treat; every day you interact with the past. Knowing that people have lived there before you and that your house is a long-standing part of the area are probably the most compelling inspirations for the majority of house restorers.

Old buildings can be connected to famous people or events. They could even, like charitable almshouses, be the physical embodiment of an important idea or philosophy. An old house could be the earliest or best example of a particular fashion in building, from daringly different modernism to the romantic Victorian Gothic.

Old buildings reveal other secrets, too. They tell us how our ancestors lived and worked, what daily life was like in the past, and what people really cared about. They show us how people earned a living, how an area's fortunes could rise and fall, and how technical progress changed the landscape. Old buildings can even tell us about the physical geography of an area. In the days before cheap transport and mass production, building materials came from the surrounding area, and we can easily deduce which types of stone, clay, wood and other materials were available locally at any time in history.

Financial advantage

Restoration projects are rarely cheap, so if you're looking for a quick return on your money, they probably aren't for you. However, there's no doubt that houses with historic interest – especially if they're listed – fetch a significantly higher price than new builds. In most cases, whatever you spend on a restoration project will add directly to the value of the house (provided, of course, you didn't overpay for the property in the first place). In some cases, you'll get back more than you've spent. As property expert Sarah Beeny puts it, 'While investing in a listed building can make property development more complicated, it can also give you a premium when it comes to selling.'

Not only that, as the owner of a restoration project, you'll probably have prospective buyers knocking down your door. Estate agents deliberately highlight any feature of historical interest – cornicing, fireplaces, dado rails, cast-iron baths, original tiles and other decorative

Preserving a building for generations to come – just one of the great benefits of a careful and sympathetic restoration job.

elements. Imagine how excited both estate agents and house-hunters get when an all-too-rare historic property with most or all of its original features comes on the market.

Ecological reasons

Old houses contain lots of embodied energy (i.e. the energy and raw materials it took to create the structure), so it makes sound ecological sense to restore a house rather than knock it down and start again. With resources getting scarcer by the day, it's sensible to reuse old buildings whenever possible. As Philip Venning, secretary for the Society for the Protection of Ancient Buildings, points out, 'Some people think a love of the old is simply about nostalgia, or write it off as a refusal to embrace the future. They couldn't be more wrong. Historic buildings give us all a sense of identity and place. We have a duty to look after them so that future generations can enjoy them. But we also have a duty to past generations not to squander the effort, money and resources they put into the buildings they left us.'

Old buildings, contrary to popular belief, are often better built and more thermo-efficient than their modern counterparts, requiring less energy to heat, cool and ventilate them. A large proportion of old houses also have inherent energy-saving features, such as thick walls and doors, small windows, well-insulated roofs and good ventilation. In addition, traditional building materials, such as lime, timber and cob, are much more environmentally friendly than modern materials, such as plastics, chrome and concrete.

Historic buildings – whether oast houses, cottages or old chapels – add aesthetic richness to the British landscape.

Personal attachment

People often have a strong connection with a particular house or building; perhaps earlier generations of their family lived or worked there. Some people find themselves living in old schools, churches or other community buildings. As historic buildings expert Pamela Cunnington notes, 'Old buildings and streets can give us a sense of continuity, stability and security.' An old house is an important heirloom, and if you're lucky enough to be the recipient of a family home in need of restoration, the process of bringing it back to life will be doubly enjoyable and rewarding.

Uniqueness

One of the criticisms of modern houses is their 'sameness'. Unimaginative suburbs and housing estates lack the distinctiveness that so many people crave. Period homes, by contrast, are often one-offs, either because they were built to be unique, or because they are the last surviving remnant of a building style. Not only are their exteriors unusual and interesting, but, as often as not, the interiors are filled with character too. Old buildings also develop a unique mellowness and charm in the same way that antique furniture acquires a wonderful patina over time.

Community spirit

If you're keen to get involved with your local community, restoring a period home is a great way to do your bit. You'll add to the historic and aesthetic richness of the area, and, in practical terms, you'll also encourage employment. When you restore a house, use local builders and craftsmen

– they invariably have a better understanding of the vernacular traditions of your region. Using traditional building methods, such as thatching, will also keep valuable skills alive for generations to come.

Thatching – one of the many vernacular building traditions currently enjoying a welcome revival.

Educational reasons

We all know that learning from textbooks can be a bit dry. History best comes to life when taught with the help of visual aids and practical demonstrations. Old houses are just this – living history lessons. Students of history, archaeology, engineering, sociology, architecture, fashion – almost any subject – can learn a great deal from old structures. Being involved in a restoration project allows us to learn at first hand what works and what doesn't, what looks good, what social changes have taken place, and how building techniques, materials and styles have developed over the years.

Fun

Restoration is a thrilling, challenging and life-changing experience. It can be difficult, but the rewards are high and you'll never forget the experience. There are plenty of ups and downs in house restoration, but you'll rarely find someone who has completed a house and not been glad that he or she took up the challenge. It can also be a great way to meet new people, forge friendships and get familiar with your local area.

Feeling connected

Working on your own house makes you feel connected to your home in a way that just doesn't happen if you buy an 'off-the-shelf' property. Your

CHAUMIERE

restored home reflects the choices you've made: you're surrounded with a house that you helped to create with your own two hands. Every part of your house will tell a story.

SO WHAT KINDS OF BUILDING NEED RESTORING?

You'd be forgiven for thinking that you need to be loaded to tackle a restoration project in the UK today. Soaring house prices have put many people off even considering a period property that needs serious care and attention. Added to this, the rising cost of skilled labour and raw materials, not to mention the timescales and red tape involved, it's not surprising that potential restorers can be deterred. But they shouldn't be. As you'll see in the next chapter, it's getting easier for private individuals to raise money for restoration projects. There's also a greater number of skilled, affordable craftsmen and builders available for restoration projects if you know where to look.

All sorts of buildings need loving restoration, and not just huge country mansions and manor houses. Britain has a wealth of historic buildings, many of which have fallen into disrepair, ranging from stately piles to humble cottages. It's estimated that one important old building has been lost in the United Kingdom every day since the end of World War II. Even today, there are roughly 20,000 historic buildings and monuments still at risk.

So what types of restoration projects are out there for the private individual? At the top end of the financial scale sit large country estates

Farmhouses and workers' cottages – two of the most popular choices for first-time restorers.

and manor houses. Changes in social policy and taxation, among other things, mean that most grand houses were built for a way of life that has largely died out since World War II. During the 1950s and 1960s, a shockingly large number of important country houses were demolished or neglected, their owners no longer able to afford the running costs. The National Trust and other similar bodies now own a number of these remaining properties, but can't afford to buy and maintain them all. If you have a very healthy budget, it is still possible to buy a large manor or country house to restore. Most of us, however, have to consider something a little smaller and less financially crippling.

Farmhouses and cottages are still a popular choice for would-be restorers. During the twentieth century the arrival of the car opened up the countryside to urban populations, and in recent years it's become common for city dwellers to own a second home in the countryside. This has created its own set of problems, not least pushing rural house prices beyond the means of many local residents. However, a positive side effect has been a renewed interest in preserving these humble buildings.

As the fortunes of country houses declined after the last war, so too did many of the farms and cottages that were owned by the estates, or whose occupants relied on the estates for work. In the 1960s and 1970s many farmhouses and cottages were left redundant and soon became dilapidated. Nowadays the trend has reversed: farm buildings and rural cottages are in great demand. In fact, finding one that hasn't been 'restored' is a challenge. However, many have suffered from poor-quality restorations or unsympathetic alterations, so one opportunity may lie in undoing the mistakes of previous owners. If you are lucky enough to find an unrestored farm building or cottage, it's vital (as it is with all restoration projects) that it doesn't become a pastiche of the past or an imitation of 'olde worlde country living'.

Urban properties, particularly town houses, have become increasingly popular as restoration projects. Many people find the generous proportions of Georgian and Victorian houses very pleasing, especially when the modern alternative in built-up areas is a cramped box perched on a pocket handkerchief of land. Older terraces often have better gardens, room sizes and sound insulation than newer terraced housing, making it easier to live side by side with your neighbour.

During the middle of the twentieth century it became very fashionable to cover up the ornate detailing in these houses: panelled doors were boarded over with plywood, fireplaces blocked up, colourful floor tiles hidden by carpets, and old bathrooms and kitchens replaced with new fitted designs. It's now a common pastime among the British to reverse these changes and make the most of any original features, even in modest back-to-back terraces.

Although demand is high for these types of old building, there's still a good supply of Victorian and, to a lesser extent, Georgian town houses that would benefit from a bit of sympathetic TLC. Restorers are also starting to turn their attention to later properties – Arts and Crafts, Edwardian, inter-war housing, and even those built as late as the 1960s and 1970s. It seems as if the time it takes for a building to become of historic interest is shortening by the day, especially if it is a particularly well-designed or unusual example.

Uncovering and restoring period features such as fireplaces, staircases and original tiles will attract prospective buyers and add a significant premium to your home.

Industrial buildings and factories often make exciting and unusual restoration projects, as with this builders' workshop in Walthamstow, East London.

Opportunities for restoration can also be found in buildings other than houses. Schools, hospitals, asylums, theatres, cinemas – all these structures can make exciting residential properties, but are more about conversion than restoration. One advantage of restoring such a property is that finding a new use for it probably saves it from demolition. As these buildings are often familiar landmarks, it's better that they continue in whatever form is viable, rather than have to be destroyed.

The same argument can be made for chapels and churches, a well-mined seam for would-be restorers. Around seventy ecclesiastical buildings are put on the market every year by the Church of England, Catholic and Methodist authorities. This is sometimes due to declining attendance figures, and sometimes because congregations decide that their needs are better served by a newer, larger building. Often the maintenance costs of old churches are too much for a local parish to sustain. Whatever the reason, redundant churches and chapels are snapped up as soon as they come on to the market. Keep your eyes peeled or ask around if you think this type of project might be for you because these kinds of property rarely make it to the estate agent's window.

If you're looking for a bargain restoration project (if there is such a thing in today's property market), it might be worth thinking about less conventional buildings, such as small factories, shops, mills, breweries, workshops, transport buildings – properties that were never intended to be lived in. Again, this isn't restoration in its strictest sense, but the rescuing, repairing and sympathetic conversion of an old building has to be preferable to letting it fall into rack and ruin, especially if it's of historic interest.

R.V. AMEY
BUILDER · DECORATOR · CONTRACTOR
102

One particularly interesting area of restoration is vernacular buildings. Britain is jam-packed with beautiful and varied building styles specific to a certain area – think of Cotswold limestone cottages, Kent oast houses, Devon thatched cob buildings or Norfolk dwellings faced with distinctive flint nap. Each type of regional building has its own social history, craftsmanship and mix of local building materials. In the same way that people are rediscovering the value of local food, so interest is growing in these regionally distinct buildings. (Useful Addresses on pages 245–251 provides contact details of organizations that list all sorts of buildings in need of restoration.)

HOW FAR DO YOU TAKE THE RESTORATION PROCESS?

One of the problems with restoration is working out how far to take it. While it's easy to see why modern uPVC (plastic) windows should be removed from an eighteenth-century farmhouse, for example, is it right to remove a Georgian extension from a medieval house just because it's not part of the original design?

Be aware of local building traditions in your area – are the buildings predominately stone, as with the famous Arlington Row in Bibury, Gloucestershire, *left*, or should you be using other traditional materials such as cob, handmade brick or timber?

Building specialists still disagree over this very point, and there are no simple answers. Even the terminology can't be agreed on. Some people view 'restoration' as a negative word, taking it to mean attempting to return a building to a particular date, thereby ruining its real history and character. After all, isn't it important to preserve all elements of a building's fabric and history, even those added some time after its original construction? As a result, many experts won't use the term 'restoration'; they prefer 'conservation', 'repair' or the rather vague 'care'.

Historic buildings expert Hugh Lander, however, thinks the trouble with the word 'restoration' is that it has come to imply 'over-restoration'. It all started in the eighteenth century, when a few over-zealous architects suddenly took a fancy to medieval architecture. Rather than skilfully conserve these ancient buildings, the Georgians created their own idea of what 'medieval' should look like, thereby destroying the original fabric of the structure and creating an entirely new mock-medieval style we now know as Gothick. Many Renaissance and contemporary buildings also got the same heavy-handed treatment.

A century later the fashion was still continuing. The designer William Morris, furious at what he saw happening, heavily criticized this notion of 'restoration', and in 1877 founded the Society for the Protection of Ancient Buildings (SPAB), an organization that still has a vital role in protecting Britain's built heritage. His ideas were clear: that restoration should be about simple repairs, not about trying to make a building more 'historically correct' or unnecessarily renewing old work. His ideas are still as relevant today, and form the basis of all good restoration work.

During the process of restoration, it's important to remember that just because a feature is less than 100 years old doesn't mean it's not worth preserving. As Pamela Cunnington points out in her book *Caring for Old Houses*, 'The second fifty years in the life of an old building are probably its most dangerous. It is old enough to be out of date, but not yet old enough to be considered historic.' It's only in the last few years that wartime and post-war buildings, for example, have received any serious attention.

Good restoration doesn't treat buildings in isolation; you need to be sympathetic to your surroundings and take account of the relationship of buildings to one another.

So whether or not you use the word 'restoration' is up to you. The term has become misappropriated over the years and should not be confused with over-restoration or refurbishment (ripping out old fittings and replacing them with new ones). Good restoration should be about returning a building to its former glory, not a contrived notion of the past. It should be about being true to the original spirit of the building, while respecting the changes the building has gone through.

What you don't have to do, however, is treat every change with equal weight. For instance, a poorly designed, flat-roofed extension from the 1960s does not have the same architectural importance as, say, a fine example of striking modernism. Factors such as the quality of materials and design, competence, inventiveness, consistency, legal issues and historical appreciation all come together when deciding what to keep and what to remove when restoring a property. It's not easy to make such decisions, but you can at least approach them realistically. To help you negotiate this tricky area, here are ten guidelines that any would-be restorer should follow (opposite).

BASIC RULES OF RESTORATION

1 **If it ain't broke, don't fix it.** Be as light-handed as possible with any restoration project. More damage can be done in over-restoring a property than under-restoring it.

2 **Repair, don't replace.** If an architectural feature is broken or damaged, always try to repair it rather than replace it with a new one. Not only does this make good practical and economic sense, but you're also preserving as much of the original building as possible.

3 **Follow what's already there.** If a feature is too damaged to repair, try to get as similar a replacement as possible, and try to use the same raw materials, construction techniques and design. You can either commission someone to make an item, or have a good hunt around in salvage yards. If you do visit a salvage yard, however, make sure it subscribes to the SALVO code, a set of guidelines that ensures a company's salvage comes from reliable sources. Visit www.salvo.co.uk for more information.

4 **Employ experts.** Some of the jobs on a restoration project, such as thatching or stonemasonry, should really be left to the experts. Learn when to DIY and when to call in the professionals.

5 **Use authentic materials.** Avoid modern building materials that are incompatible with the needs of old buildings. Lime putty, for example, lets an old building breathe, absorbing condensation and allowing damp to evaporate. And as lime is a relatively soft material compared to cement, it can accommodate the slight movements that traditional buildings often experience. See the 'Lime' chapter for more information.

6 **Be gentle.** Certain chemical and physical treatments, such as sandblasting, can cause damage to historical materials. Avoid these at all costs.

7 **Do your homework.** Immerse yourself in books about architectural history and techniques of building construction. You might not want to do any of the hands-on restoration yourself, but you should be knowledgeable about the subject and fully involved in the decision-making process.

8 **Research your house.** Piece together the history of your home. Maps, deeds, newspapers, old photographs, manorial court rolls, wills, tithe maps and censuses are just a few of the documents that can help you build up a picture of the architectural history and occupancy of your home. The local history section at your library, or the County Records Office, are both good places to start. There's also a wide selection of books available on tracing the history of your home.

9 **Join a society.** Membership of an organization such as SPAB or the National Trust is invaluable. Go to their meetings and lectures, meet like-minded people, visit open days at historic buildings and get advice from people in the know.

10 **Keep up a dialogue with your local Planning Department.** Whether your house is listed or not, it's important to keep up a good relationship with planning and conservation officers. See the next chapter for further information about planning and listing.

FINANCE AND PROJECT MANAGEMENT

An entire book could be written about choosing the right restoration project, but in reality your decision will be ruled as much by your heart as your head. Most people see a property, fall madly in love with it and then find a way to afford it. If this sounds like you, don't worry – a restoration project needs passion behind it – but there are a few key things you need to consider before jumping in feet first.

It goes without saying that you have to work out very carefully what you can afford, taking into account purchase price, professional fees, repairs and a healthy contingency fund (at least 10 per cent of your entire budget). As important as these upfront costs, however, is calculating whether you can afford the ongoing maintenance costs, and whether this will fit within your everyday household expenses. If you find yourself saying, 'We'll survive on baked beans and love' or 'I can always sell a kidney', you're probably overstretching yourself.

Owning a period property is like owning a classic car: you'll need to carry on ploughing money and care into it long after the restoration work has finished, or your investment will soon start losing value. Good maintenance, such as clearing out the guttering and repairing roof leaks, is always an essential part of this process, but if your building is listed and you allow it to fall into major disrepair, the local authority has the power to make you put it right.

Restoration projects can eat money. Make sure you have enough capital not just to finish the project, but to maintain the repairs for years to come.

The second important question to ask yourself is whether the building can cater for your needs. Too many people buy a teeny-weeny cottage, only to find that they don't like living in such a small space. The same applies to large, echoing spaces, such as warehouses and churches. Remember too that when buildings are radically altered or extended they can end up losing much of their original character and charm. This is not what good restoration is about. Find a property that is already the right size to fulfil your requirements.

SHOW ME THE MONEY

Few people have enough disposable cash to finance a restoration project outright. This leaves you with two options – get a mortgage and/or get a grant. We'll come to grants in a minute, but first what are your options when it comes to borrowing money from your bank?

In recent years banks and building societies have become more amenable to lending on restoration projects. The combination of high demand and a buoyant house market has encouraged high-street lenders to see restoration projects as potential money-spinners, and thus relatively safe to lend against.

On average, you can hope to increase the value of your period property by 20–30 per cent on top of whatever you spend restoring it. So, for example, if you bought a house for £100,000 and spent £50,000 on repairs, the finished article should be worth between £180,000 and £195,000.

It's what the Americans call 'sweat equity' – adding value to a property through the type of hard work that puts most people off. Making money isn't guaranteed, of course. Restoration projects are not the same as property development. Some restoration projects may only break even, while others may actually lose money, but you greatly increase your chances of success by meticulous planning, strict budgeting and tight project management.

It is only when you get behind plaster and render that you find out what the restoration will really cost.

Mortgages

Getting a mortgage on a restoration project isn't as simple as getting a mortgage on a standard property. This is largely because the bank or building society has to lend money on something that won't realize its equity until it's finished. There's also a greater risk for the lender that the buyer will default on the mortgage, leaving an unsaleable wreck behind.

Certain companies, however, are prepared to lend you the money. Some building societies offer so-called 'green mortgages'. The Ecology Building Society, for example, funds mortgage lending on a number of eco-friendly projects, including energy-efficient housing, ecological renovation and derelict, dilapidated properties. Not only do restoration projects count as 'derelict and dilapidated', but many of the traditional building materials you will use in your project are environmentally preferable. Be sure to point this out if you plan to apply for a green mortgage on a restoration project.

There are also 'brown mortgages'. The Norwich and Peterborough Building Society offers this type of mortgage to encourage people to build on brownfield sites or to do up redundant properties rather than build on virgin land, as many self-builders tend to do.

It's also worth sweet-talking your existing lender. Many of the bigger banks are prepared to lend on unfinished properties, especially if they are habitable. In practice, this means that the property will need to have a functioning roof, a basic kitchen and bathroom, running water and a power supply. It will be up to you to convince the bank that this project will be a success, so back up your case with lots of plans, quotes and confident smiles.

LEFT In Grafham House, Surrey, work didn't begin until the roof was fixed – a golden rule of restoration.

RIGHT Restoration mortgages are often released in stages. Remedial structural work, like these roof repairs on a seventeenth-century Suffolk school, should come first.

Whichever mortgage you choose, you need to be aware that the money will usually be released only in stages after essential works have been done. You'll be expected to carry out structural work and emergency repairs first – subsidence, damp, dry rot and suchlike – before starting to choose lovely taps and curtain rails. At each stage a surveyor will visit the property to check that the work has been carried out to a sufficient standard before any money is released.

There's one obvious flaw with this course of events: you have to provide the money upfront to pay for any repairs. It's important, therefore, to have sufficient funds in reserve to cover the initial stage of the building process until the mortgage company effectively pays you back.

At the time of writing there is something called an 'accelerator mortgage', which gets round this problem by releasing the money in agreed amounts upfront. So instead of providing funds in arrears as each building stage is completed, the lender releases money *before* each stage of work starts. Building societies manage this by adding indemnity insurance to your mortgage, to protect them against lending on an asset that doesn't yet exist. Several lenders offer this type of product, so ask an independent financial adviser or mortgage broker for more details.

If you apply for a restoration mortgage, you may have to provide detailed plans of any building works along with a proposed time schedule. These are just to reassure the lender that you have thought seriously about how the work will progress. At the very minimum, provide the lender with a proposed schedule of works, estimates based on actual quotes and a deadline for the end of the project. It doesn't matter if deadlines change

R. HOGG & SON

over the course of the project (which they undoubtedly will), as long as you keep up a good dialogue with your lender.

Be aware, however, that some lenders put time limits on any works that need completing. Miss that deadline and you may find yourself having to reapply for a mortgage halfway through your project – not ideal. As soon as you finish your restoration project, switch back to a normal mortgage – you'll find that restoration mortgages usually come with a higher rate of interest.

Grants

Restoration grants, especially for private individuals, are as rare as hens' teeth. Never ever rely on a grant to fund your restoration project, but if you know who to approach, and take the time to make a compelling case, who knows ... you might just get lucky.

The best place to start your search for a grant is the Architectural Heritage Fund on the Funds for Historic Buildings website (see page 245). This is a free online guide to all the different types of funding currently available in the UK.

To keep costs down, Val and Les at Higher Hill Farm, Lancashire, *left*, lived on site in caravans, whilst Brian and Nigel at Biddulph, Staffordshire, *right*, rushed through a couple of rooms to provide a bolt hole to live in. How you occupy your house during the works will significantly affect the experience.

Most grants are conditional, in the sense that the benefactor will want work to be carried out in a certain way. English Heritage, for example, requires any restoration work to be 'sympathetic to the character and importance of the building, site or landscape'. It will also expect repairs to be of a high standard, the building to be well maintained and, in some cases, a certain level of public access to the building once the work has been completed. This doesn't necessarily mean that you'll have to turn your home into a visitors' attraction complete with gift shop and tearoom, but it might mean the odd open day or educational visit.

If you delve further into the Architectural Heritage Fund database, you'll also find grants that encourage restoration projects with an environmental or rural component, or discover small pockets of money assigned to projects that support inner-city regeneration, disabled access and multi-occupancy projects. Try to think imaginatively about whether any of these grants could fit with your aims and objectives.

Local authority Historic Building Grants are also available to the owners of old houses at the discretion of the council. They usually cover modest sums (between £1000 and £10,000) and are designed to help with the repair of traditional buildings within a specific local authority. A condition of grant funding is often the use of traditional building materials and techniques. Historic Building Grants frequently go to listed buildings of special architectural or historic interest, but money is also awarded to non-listed buildings, especially if they are in prominent public view or a designated conservation area. Contact the conservation officer in the Planning Department at your local authority for more information.

Tax relief

What is it they say about death and taxes? Well, the latter is not a certainty in this case. It's worth knowing that although VAT is payable on all repairs to buildings, if your restoration project is listed, you shouldn't have to pay VAT on approved alterations (those that comply with listed building consent). This may seem counterintuitive to the whole idea of restoration – that it should be about repairing and retaining the character of a building, not altering it – but the words 'gift horse' and 'mouth' spring to mind.

To help you make sense of this complex area, the Society for the Protection of Ancient Buildings has produced a helpful booklet entitled 'VAT and Historic Buildings, SPAB Guide 1' (see page 249).

Did someone famous live in your house? English Heritage's blue plaques mark the homes of the famous. John Lennon lived in this 1930s semi in Liverpool.

LISTED BUILDINGS

Fancy living in a listed building? Before you take the plunge it's vital to know just what makes a building listed and what it will mean for you. The Department for Culture, Media and Sport, with the assistance of English Heritage, has created a list of buildings with special historic or architectural interest. This list, which now has more than 370,000 entries, includes large, impressive buildings, such as castles and cathedrals, as well as smaller domestic properties, monuments, follies and commercial buildings across England. About 40 per cent of these are private homes.

The buildings are divided into three categories. Grade I are of exceptional interest. Grade II* are particularly important buildings of more than special interest, and Grade II are of special interest. Most of the

ENGLISH HERITAGE
JOHN
LENNON
1940-1980
Musician
and Songwriter
lived here
1945-1963

buildings on the list are classed as Grade II. (The Scottish listing system uses grades A, B and C, which have similar meanings to the English ones, and Northern Ireland has grades A, B+, B1 and B2.)

As a rule of thumb, the older a building, the more likely it is to get listed. In England all pre-1700 buildings that survive in anything like their original condition are listed, as are most of those built between 1700 and 1840. At the other end of the timescale, post-1945 buildings have to be of exceptional importance to be listed.

If you want to find out whether a building is protected, pop into your nearest library or planning office and ask for the local list. A nationwide list is kept at the National Monuments Record Centre in Swindon, but you can also try Images of England, a digital library of photographs of England's listed buildings (see page 248).

Listed building consent

The purpose of listing is to protect historic buildings from harm. Therefore, if a building is listed, you have to get 'listed building consent' before most works are carried out. This applies to both outside and inside alterations, and even to relatively minor jobs, such as repainting or putting up a TV aerial.

Sympathetic repairs don't usually need listed building consent, but this is a grey area, so *always* check with the conservation officer at your local council before you do anything. An informal chat with him or her will help to establish whether your ideas will even be considered. Once you have a better idea of the rules and regulations, make an official application; you can get a form from the Planning Department.

Buildings don't have to be ancient to be listed, as London's striking Barbican Centre demonstrates.

With your application include as much information as possible, showing clearly what you want to achieve. Detailed plans and photographs will help your case. If you plan to carry out major works, it's useful to get help from an architect used to dealing with listed buildings.

If you own a listed building, you should be aware that you're not allowed to let it fall into disrepair. John Yates, an English Heritage inspector, offers the following advice:

> 'While there is no set legal duty to maintain a listed building, if it is seriously neglected, the local planning authority can serve two kinds of notice on the owner. They are in the Planning (Listed Buildings and Conservation Areas) Act 1990. In Section 54 of that Act is the Urgent Works Notice, which can be served only on empty buildings, and requires the owner to carry out urgent minimum works to make the building stable, weathertight and secure. This will often just be temporary works, such as propping up a wall or putting a sheet over a roof. If the work isn't done, the council can go in and do it, and charge the owner.
>
> 'In Section 48 is the Repairs Notice, which requires full repairs, and can lead to compulsory purchase by the council. In fact, compulsory purchase rarely happens because the threat alone is usually enough to concentrate the mind of the owner. Guidance on all of this is in the government's 'Policy Planning Guidance Note 15', the conservation officer's bible, which can be found on the Office of the Deputy Prime Minister's website.'

LEFT Grafham House, Surrey, was listed and a late application for listed-building consent nearly caused the whole build to grind to a halt.

RIGHT Sometimes a whole street will be listed.

Owners of listed buildings will also find the Listed Property Owners' Club (see page 248) a useful source of information and advice on many different aspects of the process, including your legal responsibilities and obligations, guidance on grants and loans, planning advice and property maintenance.

Note: A complete overhaul of the listing system was outlined in a government consultation paper in July 2004, so keep an eye out for any changes that might affect you from April 2005.

Getting a building listed

If you feel you have a building that should be listed but isn't, draw the government's attention to it by writing to the Listing Team (see page 248).

English Heritage advises that in any correspondence to the Listing Team you should include a clear outline of your reasons why the building needs listing, as well as:

- A location plan showing, wherever possible, the position of any other listed buildings nearby
- Clear, up-to-date photographs of the main elevations of the building
- Any information about the building, e.g. date
- Details of specialized function, e.g. industrial use
- Historical associations
- The name of the architect
- The building's group value in the street scene
- Details of any interior features of interest
- The daytime telephone number of the owner or his or her agent who may be able to give access to the building for an inspection

Priority treatment will be given to those buildings that are under immediate threat, but you can help your case by getting the support of a respected historical or conservation group.

CALLING IN THE PROFESSIONALS

You won't be able to do everything yourself, so you'll have to call on professional help. The first professional to cross your path in any restoration project will be a surveyor. Your mortgage company can lend you money only on the strength of the building being worth what you say it is. Unless you ask for something different, the lender's surveyor will come and do a basic valuation survey only.

There are two problems with this. First, your average surveyor will not be experienced in old buildings, so they may be alarmed by the state of the property and undervalue it. Second, this type of survey tells you very little about the condition of the building.

Given these drawbacks, it is best to get a full structural survey from a surveyor who is familiar with old buildings. That way you'll know what you're really buying, warts and all. Even though it will cost you more than a basic valuation – around £1000, as opposed to £250 – it is money well spent.

Get it done properly. There are certain jobs on a restoration project, including stonemasonry, woodturning and decorative plasterwork, that are best left to the professionals.

Finding a surveyor

The Royal Institution of Chartered Surveyors (RICS, see page 249) has a list of conservation-friendly surveyors who will be properly able to assess the problems of an old building and reassure a concerned mortgage company. They, unlike many standard surveyors, will also suggest remedies compatible with an old building for common problems such as rising damp. In this case, rather than the 'modern' solution, which is to install a chemical or electric damp-proof course around the base of the walls, they would suggest less intrusive or destructive methods, such as a French drain (a small trench that allows surface water to drain away) or better ventilation.

Finding an architect and builder

After your survey has been done and you've decided you want to get cracking, the next stage is to call in an architect and/or a builder. Either of these professionals can also project-manage on your behalf if you decide not to do it yourself. The role of the project manager is probably the most important on the site. He or she is responsible for the smooth running of the project, which involves dealing with tradesmen, ordering materials,

At Heolas Fawr in Wales, Mary Jane and Gervase did just about everything themselves. It saved them money but made progress extremely slow.

checking building regulations, troubleshooting and scheduling all the work so that nothing clashes. Expect to spend up to 10 per cent of the total budget on a project manager. It might seem like a lot of money, but project-managing is a particularly demanding, stressful and time-consuming role.

It's vital that you employ professionals who are knowledgeable about old buildings. The best place to start is *The Building Conservation Directory*: you can either buy the book or search for companies on the website (see page 246). Period Property and SPAB also have extensive lists of appropriate specialists (see pages 248–9 for all contact details).

For an architect conversant in restoration issues, have a look at the Royal Institute of British Architect's UK Directory of Registered Practices, which can be found on their website (www.riba.org) or the Register of Architects Accredited in Building Conservation (see page 249).

It's extremely important to find a conservation builder you can trust. Start by asking friends, family and other period property owners for recommendations: you'll be getting an honest appraisal from someone whose opinion you trust. Don't forget to ask about the builder's conduct, as well as the quality of the workmanship.

Contact respected trade bodies and builders' associations to get a list of registered members. The Federation of Master Builders (see page 247), for example, has around 13,000 building firms on its books, all of whom have signed up to its strict code of practice. The government's Quality Mark logo is also a useful indicator of a reputable building company.

The conservation officer at your council will, of course, have a good idea of local companies who specialize in heritage work, as will historical building societies in your area. If you're really struggling to get any recommendations, contact the enquiries desk at a local historic landmark and ask who does that building's maintenance and building work.

Once you have a prospective builder, ask for two or three references from previous clients, and follow them up. Even better, go and see the work for yourself. If you're satisfied, the next step is to get quotes – ideally from two or three different builders, although this can be tricky with so few conservation-friendly builders to choose from. Be sure to ask for quotes, not estimates. Estimates for work have a funny way of increasing once a job has been completed. A written quote, on the other hand, is legally binding once accepted, and shouldn't change. This is very desirable, especially if you're really watching the pennies.

Once the figures have been agreed, draw up a contract. This is for the benefit of both parties and helps to clarify what's expected over the course of the project. For a big restoration project, make sure the contract includes not only dates and costs, but also specifies toilet facilities, waste disposal, working hours and other areas that are part and parcel of a building job. Download a free domestic building contract at the Federation of Master Builders' website (see page 247).

As part of the contract, you'll also need to clarify the arrangements for insurance. Your builder should have a public liability insurance certificate, but you'll also need to check whether your own insurance policy is affected by the building work.

BUILDING MATERIALS

There's good reason for following traditional practices in your restoration project. Until relatively recently, old buildings were mended and maintained using modern building materials, such as plastics and concrete. While these materials have their own merits, their use on period properties isn't always wise. Carl Carrington, architectural historian and conservation consultant at Carrington Associates, explains why: 'If you start using modern materials on traditional constructions, you don't always know how they are going to behave. We know that traditional building materials, such as lime and timber, are flexible enough to accommodate the movements that old buildings experience over time. They're also in keeping with the original fabric of the building, and will weather gently over time. In some circumstances, it can be appropriate to use modern materials on old structures, or there are instances where the costs of using traditional building materials are prohibitively high, but these cases are generally the exception rather than the rule.'

It's interesting to note that some of the worst examples of poor restoration have occurred over the last few decades, with the arrival of 'modern miracles', such as uPVC windows, strong cement mortars and vinyl paints. As you will see in this section, using traditional building materials and techniques can involve a bit more research, effort or money than their modern equivalents. What will also become apparent, however, is that by using authentic materials you are not only preserving the character of your house, but you are also choosing longevity over quick-fix repairs that will ultimately destroy the very house you are trying to restore.

An added benefit to learning about traditional building methods will be your ability to deal with tradesmen and builders confidently. Many people who take on restoration projects say that they often feel railroaded into certain decisions because they don't have the background knowledge to ask for what they really want. This is often true with the building profession, where each different tradesman has his own method of doing a job and is reluctant to see any alternatives. Getting builders to use lime mortar instead of cement, for example, is a challenge in itself, and best taken on only after you've armed yourself with the facts. At the end of the day, you should be in charge of your project, and anyone you employ should be working to your specifications. That said, diplomacy and tact will always get you much further with experienced tradesmen than a dictatorial approach.

But this section isn't just about running a restoration project from the sidelines. In the following chapters there are also a number of practical things you'll be able to tackle yourself – from simple tasks suitable for people with no previous restoration experience to more complicated jobs for the competent DIYer.

LIME

Ask any conservation builder about lime and you'll see his eyes shine with joy. Builders love it, and so should you. Lime has been used as a building material for thousands of years – the Egyptians were plastering their buildings with it as early as 4000 BC – and we even have an early recipe for lime mortar from the famous Roman architect Vitruvius. During the late nineteenth century, with the rise of new materials such as Portland cement, lime fell out of favour, but in recent years it has been enjoying something of a revival among house restorers. This is fantastic news because, as you shall see later, lime is one of the most versatile and healthy materials for old buildings. Few people outside conservation circles, however, know what it is or how to use it.

HERE COMES THE SCIENCE...

Two very different uses of lime: *left*, as a flexible and breathable finish on a timber-framed house and, *above right*, as a medium for intricate decorative plasterwork.

The way we make lime hasn't changed for centuries. Lumps of limestone (calcium carbonate) are fired in a kiln to around 900°C (1650°F) to produce a highly reactive substance called quicklime (calcium oxide). The heating process drives off lots of carbon dioxide, leaving the lime much lighter in weight. Water is then added to the quicklime, which causes a violent chemical reaction. The mixture bubbles furiously and produces heat well above boiling point, a process know as 'slaking'. (Limestone is a sedimentary stone derived from the remains of sea organisms and shells. In the past, when limestone wasn't available, builders could create quicklime by burning seashells in a kiln.)

After the lime has been slaked and the mixture has cooled down, it will look like thick-set double cream. This is 'lime putty' (calcium hydroxide), and is the basis for many different lime products, including mortars, limewashes, renders and plaster. Like a good cheese, the lime putty needs to be left to mature for at least three months, and can be stored in sealed tubs almost indefinitely.

It is also possible to make a hot lime mix, which is suitable for mortar and plasterwork (but not for the final coat of plaster because it may contain lumps of unslaked lime). This process cuts out the lime putty phase, and is produced simply by mixing quicklime with sand and water in one go. Like lime putty, hot lime mix also needs to be left to mature.

After you've applied lime and left it to set, it slowly reabsorbs carbon dioxide from the air, to form calcium carbonate, and gradually hardens, a process known as carbonation. The result is chemically the same as the raw material you started with (limestone), but has very different physical properties.

There are two other types of lime, with confusingly similar names, that also need a mention: hydrated lime and hydraulic lime.

Hydrated lime

Also known as dry bagged lime, hydrated lime comes in powder form and is used for increasing the alkalinity of garden soil, as well as in modern mortar mixes. When mixed with water, hydrated lime produces a lime putty of sorts, but it's not as good as proper lime putty. Janet Collings, author of *Old House Care and Repair*, says that hydrated lime is to lime

ABOVE Limewash – the ultimate natural paint – breathable, inexpensive, eco-friendly and beautiful to look at.

putty as dried milk is to bottled milk, i.e. when mixed with water, it makes a passable but noticeably inferior version of the genuine article. Best to stick to the real stuff, if possible.

Hydraulic lime

Unlike normal lime putty, hydraulic lime does not need dry, airy conditions to set properly. It is made from special types of limestone that contain natural impurities, and it is these impurities that allow the lime to set quickly and in wet conditions, rather than relying on air. This is a great bonus when working in rainy weather, or building a structure under water, such as a lock or dam. The same applies to structures that are permanently damp, such as foundations.

There are several types of hydraulic lime, and they tend to be stronger and less flexible than non-hydraulic lime, behaving more like modern cement. The strength of hydraulic limes ranges from 'feebly hydraulic' (the weakest) to 'eminently hydraulic' (the strongest).

You can also artificially create a hydraulic lime by adding ingredients called 'pozzolans' to normal lime putty. These ingredients include things such as volcanic ash, pumice and brick dust, and the process is known as 'gauging'.

With both natural hydraulic limes and pozzolan mixes, what you gain in strength you lose in flexibility and permeability. In general, conservationists tend to stay away from the strongest hydraulic limes and use either non-hydraulic lime (lime putty) or feebly to moderately hydraulic limes.

LEFT Seventeenth-century plasterwork at the former Sun Inn in Saffron Walden, Essex.

RIGHT Old timber-framed buildings, such as these Tudor shops in Suffolk, move and warp with the seasons; lime plaster and mortar can accommodate these natural movements.

SAFETY NOTE

Quicklime is highly caustic and will burn on contact with your skin (hence its use in the Middle Ages to disinfect and dissolve the corpses of those who had died from the Black Death). When handling quicklime or tackling the slaking process, always wear waterproof protective clothing, gloves, industrial footwear and safety goggles. Keep a supply of clean water close by in case of accidents, but if any quicklime gets in your eyes, seek hospital treatment immediately.

WHY USE LIME?

There are lots of reasons to use lime in a restoration project, not least that it is relatively soft and flexible. Old buildings tend to move, they often have shallow foundations, and are made from materials such as timber and handmade brick that expand and contract with the seasons. Unlike cement, lime can accommodate the slight movements that traditional buildings experience. In fact, small cracks in lime will often miraculously heal themselves over time, a process known as 'autogenous healing'.

Old buildings often don't have a damp-proof course (the layer of waterproof membrane that stops ground-level moisture seeping up into the building), so they need to be able to breathe and shed water. Newer building materials, such as Portland cement, tend to trap moisture, whereas lime absorbs condensation and allows damp to evaporate out. This is vital in old buildings, as water retention can cause serious long-term structural problems.

LADY STREET

LEFT External lime render was added to old buildings as a means of extra waterproofing and insulation.

RIGHT A stone wall repointed with lime mortar, as is often required on the restoration of listed buildings.

Lime is also a joy to live with. Lime plasters feel cool in summer and warm in winter, and have a soft finish that better suits the gentle curves and contours of old buildings. Lime is also hygienic: it's a natural disinfectant and inhibits the growth of bacteria. Wood-boring beetles hate it.

WHAT CAN I DO WITH LIME?

Over the years lime has been used in almost every part of the building process, but there are four common ways you'll see lime putty used today.

Lime mortar

This is the ideal substance for bedding and jointing old walls. The usual mix is 3:1 sand to lime putty, but this can vary, depending on the quality and nature of the raw materials.

When you build or repoint an old wall it's always important that the mortar is softer than the brick or stone. This allows the mortar to act as a cushion, taking the weight of the wall and allowing slight movements. Lime mortar will also draw moisture out of the wall, allowing damp to evaporate from the building. If a mortar is harder than the brick or stone it surrounds, the brick or stone will be damaged before the mortar when the wall expands and contracts. Cement mortar, on the other hand, is very hard and designed for modern buildings, which are much more predictable and rigid.

Another benefit of lime mortar is that it is easy to remove from bricks when the building is no longer needed. This means that handmade bricks,

which are packed with character and charm (and expensive to buy), can be reused almost indefinitely, or salvaged at a future point in time. Cement mortar is a nightmare to remove once set.

Fine examples of pargeting from Clare, Suffolk, *above*, and Saffron Walden, Essex, *right*. Pargeting is a form of traditional decoration that uses lime plaster reinforced with dung, hair or hay.

Renders and plasters

These are the traditional coatings for external and internal walls respectively. External lime render was added to old buildings as a means of extra weatherproofing, or as an additional layer of insulation. It also gave the plasterer the opportunity to add some fancy decoration to the outside of a building.

Medieval timber-framed buildings often had external panels of woven chestnut, willow or hazel twigs (wattle), which were covered in daub – usually a mixture of local clay, chalk and mud. This was then finished with lime render and three or four coats of limewash. In many parts of the country the limewash was tinted with ochre or umber to give a warm, subtle colour.

External lime render continued to be the norm well into the nineteenth century. In fact, if your building pre-dates about 1850, the original render is almost certain to be made from non-hydraulic lime or feebly hydraulic lime. Portland cement, on the other hand, was patented in 1824 and only widely available from around 1845. Even after that date, many buildings still used lime render, so you'll need to check which material was used if you plan to make a like-for-like repair.

Like lime mortar, lime render can cope with tiny structural movements, as well as letting water evaporate away from the wall. Modern

Wealthy homes were often decorated with elaborate cornicing, cast ornaments and freehand stucco.

cement renders, on the other hand, are wholly inappropriate for old buildings. They crack and let in water, which then cannot escape, thus putting the fabric of the building in jeopardy.

Moving from the outside of a period property to the inside, you often find lime plaster in abundance. The current fashion is to leave internal brick and stonework uncovered, but in medieval and Tudor times this wouldn't have been the case. Interior walls would be plastered with lime, then finished with a good few coats of limewash. In wealthier houses the lime plaster was often patterned to imitate high-quality stone or timber framing, or decoratively painted with flowers or religious figures. Subsequent applications of limewash often covered up these paintings, but a skilled restorer may be able to remove the later layers of limewash to reveal the original artwork beneath.

Lime plaster was also used to cover internal partitions between rooms. These partitions would be made from woven wattle panels similar to those used on the external walls. This tradition continued well into the eighteenth century, when wattle was largely superseded by narrow strips of timber known as 'laths'. Lath and lime plaster was also used to cover ceilings.

The modern convention with plastering is to use plasterboard and gypsum plaster. This is not authentic for a historic building, as plasterboard wasn't widespread until the middle of the twentieth century, and modern bagged gypsum powders are too brittle and hard to cope with any inevitable movement in the walls. Gypsum also disintegrates in the presence of moisture, while modern water-resistant gypsum plasters lack breathability.

As with lime mortar, the mix for both lime render and lime plaster is usually 3:1 sand to lime putty (although final coats of lime plaster can range from 3:1 to 1:3 sand to lime putty). Ancient samples of lime render and lime plaster, however, show just how varied and inventive this mix could be. Sometimes animal hair (usually goat or ox) was added to the mix to reduce cracking and add strength. The quantity of hair could vary from a few tufts to 'such an abundance that sheets of plaster can literally be rolled up like a carpet without significant damage', according to conservation builder Ian Constantinides. The finish, whether rough, smooth or patterned, was dictated by the status or vernacular tradition of the area.

SAFETY NOTE

There have been scare stories in the past about the possibility of catching the potentially deadly disease anthrax from the animal hair in old plaster. The theory is that anthrax spores are extremely persistent and can be inhaled in dust from historic plaster that contains contaminated animal hair. In reality, there have been *no* recorded cases of anthrax being contracted via hair-reinforced plaster, and any risk is considered to be 'extremely unlikely' by the Centre for Applied Microbiology and Research.

However, if you are employing workmen to handle old plaster, you are bound by law to introduce appropriate health and safety measures to minimize any risk. English Heritage has a helpful leaflet called 'Anthrax and Historic Plaster', which you can download from their website, or you can contact the Health and Safety Executive (HSE) for their booklet 'Anthrax: Safe Working and the Prevention of Infection' (see page 247).

Limewash doesn't have to be white – you can add natural pigments to produce a wide range of colours, including warm reds, creams and pinks.

Limewash

This is a brilliantly simple and cheap way to paint your external and internal walls, while allowing them to 'breathe'. Simply dilute lime putty with water to get limewash, but if you don't want to make it yourself, it can be bought ready-made. Limewash is transparent when applied, but dries to a matt white/cream shade. You can also add powdered pigments to get a wide range of colours. In the past, pigments were often derived from the earth, giving rise to the warm, attractive colours we associate with old buildings, such as burnt sienna and golden ochre.

Binders, such as fats, oils and glues, can be added to limewash to increase its water-shedding properties, or reduce its tendency to brush off (although this shouldn't happen if the limewash is of good quality and properly applied). Unfortunately, the addition of binders can have the effect of reducing the breathability of limewash or, in the case of glue, increase the likelihood of mould growth. If you use limewash, you'll need to reapply it every five years or so.

Limewash can be painted over lime plaster or render, earth walls, limestone, timber and most old limewash. Unfortunately, it takes less well to cement render, plasterboard and emulsion, and is entirely unsuitable for impervious materials, such as flint and modern bricks. You'll need to contact the supplier of your limewash to check its suitability for your project.

From the Middle Ages until the eighteenth century all sorts of buildings were limewashed on both the outside and inside, from humble cottages to large buildings of national importance. The White Tower at the Tower of

LEFT The plasterwork at Bedford House in Scotland captured Mike and Mandy's hearts. Be aware that damaged plasterwork can be very expensive to fix.

RIGHT Intricate plasterwork by the plasterer John Papworth in the Book Room at Wimpole Hall, Cambridgeshire.

London, for example, is thought to have derived its name from being regularly limewashed. In the eighteenth century distemper paint began to replace limewash on the inside of grand houses, and only a century later the fashion for external limewash also started to wane. Consequently, many people removed limewash from the exterior of their houses, and only in rural areas did the popularity of limewash really remain.

Decorative plasterwork

Plasterwork was once a popular surface decoration both inside and out. In wealthy houses during the sixteenth and seventeenth centuries it was common to see heavily decorated ceilings with elaborate cornicing, moulded panels, cast ornaments and freehand stucco (raised patterns and shapes). Gypsum was often added to decorative lime plaster to extend the workability of the mix and thus allow the plasterer time to create fabulous designs. Fine marble dust was another common addition to lime plaster, and helped the plasterer to achieve a highly polished surface.

When fibrous plaster was patented in 1856 it had a significant effect on decorative plasterwork. Before this time, most decorative plasterwork was created *in situ*, either by hand or cast in small hardwood moulds. The introduction of fibrous plaster (large sections of decorative plasterwork reinforced with fabric) meant that plaster decorations could be made en masse in a workshop and then carried on to the site at a later date. This had a devastating effect on the craftsmen who traditionally created decorative plasterwork by hand, but also had the effect of making it much cheaper for the average householder to obtain.

Lime analysis

As mentioned earlier, building materials made with lime often include other ingredients, such as gypsum, sand, glue and hair. If you are repairing a house that used lime in some way in the past, it's really important to try to match the material like for like. If you have to repair a piece of historic cornicing, for example, it's always best to establish whether the original lime plaster contained gypsum. In the past, building traditions varied wildly up and down the country, so there isn't one rule that covers all lime repair work. Plasterers often had their own tried-and-trusted methods, using additives and aggregates in unusual and surprising ways.

One solution is to get a specialist firm to carry out a chemical analysis on the material you want to repair or replace. They will look at the composition of the lime mix and be able to tell you about any ingredients that were added, such as gypsum, pozzolans and binders. They may also be able to offer clues about how and when the lime was applied. This kind of specialist advice is critical if you are working on a building of national importance, but is also becoming more widely practised by regional house restorers, who want to use building materials that are as authentic as possible.

GETTING STUCK IN

Talking of expert advice, just how much of this lime work can you do yourself? That's a difficult question to answer, and one that will depend largely on the amount of skill and free time you have. However, even the most experienced builder should take a lime course before attempting

In many old houses cornicing and other pieces of plasterwork have been ripped out. A conservation plasterer will be able to match and replace any missing pieces.

restoration work of this kind. You will find short lime courses all over the country, and they will give you a good grounding in the basic theory and techniques. Take care, however, to choose a course that has a hands-on component. York University Archaeology Department, for example, runs a course where you get to lime-plaster a genuine medieval A-frame building.

Limewashing is straightforward and can be attempted by most competent DIYers. You can mix the lime putty, pigments and water yourself, but you need to be aware that colour matching is almost impossible, so you have to make enough limewash to cover the entire job in one go. You can also buy coloured, ready-made limewash, which might be a good option if you are using it for the first time. It's vital to damp down the walls with a hand-pump spray before applying the limewash to help with adhesion, but use a light touch: the wall shouldn't be running with water.

As for lime mortar, render and plaster, it's best to get professional guidance at the very least. The skills needed for applying lime render and plaster are not the same as for applying modern cement or gypsum-based products because the mixes, equipment, techniques and drying times all differ. Either consult a lime expert, who will be able to supervise the process, or, better still, employ a lime specialist on the project.

Replacing missing ornamental plasterwork, such as cornicing or stucco, is especially tricky because the work may need to be completed *in situ* or cast and fixed into place. Either way, a competent conservation plasterer is a must.

You can find details of lime experts on the websites for *The Building Conservation Directory*, Period Property and SPAB (see pages 246–249).

LEFT This yeoman's house, with its open windows and lack of chimney, shows that even homes of the wealthy were simple.

RIGHT Great Chalfield Manor in Wiltshire would have been the largest house for miles around.

THE MEDIEVAL HOUSE (pre-1500)

At the end of the medieval period, following the accession of the Tudors in 1485, the majority of British people still lived in small, cramped timber-framed houses. Wood was by far the easiest building material to source – the country was still swathed in 1.6 million hectares (4 million acres) of dense woodland – and even the most amateur builder could cut, shape and erect a wooden shelter. Except in areas where rubble stone was freely available, stone tended to be used in limited quantities or saved for the most prestigious homes.

Oak and elm were the best woods for building purposes, and medieval England was lucky enough to have a rich supply of both. That's not to say they were always affordable, though. Poorer families often had to make do with inferior, less durable woods, which is why so little medieval peasant housing has survived; that, and the fact that low-grade housing was often crudely built and rarely lasted more than a generation.

The medieval houses that do still exist were the best and most expensive, which skews our perspective of the past. Of the handful of pre-1500 buildings that survive intact, the vast majority, such as Great Chalfield in Wiltshire, belonged to wealthy merchants or landed gentry. The size, layout and quality of materials were much grander than in run-of-the-mill medieval houses, and it's important to remember that for most people in this period, home would have been a much simpler construction.

So what were peasant medieval houses like? While Gothic cathedrals were soaring into the sky, built from high-quality stone and exquisite stained glass, everyday buildings from the period were almost entirely constrained by function and the availability of building materials. The most basic form of medieval house design was the cruck house. The skeleton frame of the building consisted of pairs of arched tree trunks – think of the shape of an upturned boat – and many people today make the common mistake of assuming that these curved timbers were taken from old ships. This bowed timber frame supported the entire weight of the roof, allowing the walls to be in-filled with locally

acquired wattle-and-daubed timber panels, rubble stone or cob (a mixture of chalk, mud and straw that sets hard). The building would then often be protected with lime render and given a final coat of limewash.

Inside this simple one-room shelter, a medieval peasant ate, slept and shared his living space with his livestock. Rudimentary partitions or a mezzanine level gave him and his family an area to sleep, while a central hearth provided the only heat, smoke rising from the fire and finding its way through a straw, heather or brushwood roof.

The box-framed house was another popular style during the medieval period. A successor to the cruck design, the box frame had roof trusses supported by posts, tie-beams and wall plates. Put simply, instead of the tent-like frame of the cruck house, the box frame was exactly that – a square or rectangular box constructed from timbers. Again the walls were in-filled using wattle-and-daubed timber panels, stone or cob.

This method of construction had one great advantage over the cruck house: you could build more than one storey high. It wasn't uncommon to have a two-storey box-framed house where the upper storey overhung the one below – a style known as 'jettying'. A jettied second storey not only gave the lower part of the building some protection from driving rain and wind, but it also provided a little extra floor space upstairs.

If you want to get a more accurate understanding of what houses of this period were really like, it is worth visiting one of the building museums scattered around Britain. Places such as the Weald and Downland Museum in East Sussex or the Ryedale Folk Museum in North Yorkshire are treasure

FAR LEFT The long house, like this example at Little Langdale, Cumbria, is one of the simplest types of medieval house.

LEFT This Wealdon house in Bignor, Sussex, was typical of many houses in the southeast of England during the medieval period.

BELOW RIGHT A beautiful example of box-framed, jettied construction, here with shallow oriel windows.

troves for anyone interested in medieval domestic architecture. They contain buildings that have been dismantled piece by piece, moved to the museum and reconstructed to their original configurations using traditional methods. Getting up close to these authentic medieval buildings highlights their simplicity and ingenuity, and they contain important lessons for restorers.

As we know, medieval houses, through necessity, were built using local natural materials, such as timber, lime and cob. These materials, despite seeming rustic and unsophisticated, contain far fewer toxins or pollutants than many of our modern building materials. They move and breathe with the building, creating better internal air quality and healthier homes. They can also, despite their biodegradable qualities, outlast their modern cousins by centuries.

Locally acquired materials contain less 'embodied energy' – the energy that it takes to extract, process and transport a material to its final destination. Many of the materials in question, such as mud or rubble stone, can be obtained from within a short distance of a building project, in stark contrast to the imported stone, heavily processed plastic and energy-hungry concrete we use today.

All these factors give a good indication of why we are currently seeing a renaissance in both timber framing and the use of mud, lime and other natural materials in restoration projects. Mixing a bit of modern and medieval know-how offers a viable and intelligent approach at a time when the needs of the environment demand us to think again. It seems as if the ideas and materials of our medieval forefathers are becoming just as relevant today as they were 600 years ago.

TIMBER

The British have a lot to thank the humble tree for. From medieval times, timber was the material of choice for some of the country's most impressive monasteries and royal residences, as well as being the backbone of many small domestic dwellings and farm buildings – and with good reason. Timber makes the perfect structural building material: it holds up well under compression and tension; it's wonderfully flexible while being immensely strong; it's also ecologically friendly, beautiful to look at and easy to work with.

In medieval times timber-framed buildings were the order of the day. They ranged in complexity from crude, single-storey post-and-beam houses to complicated A-framed and box-framed buildings complete with upper floors that often extended out into the street. Some of the country's most beautiful domestic examples of jettied timber-framed buildings still survive today in places such as York and Ludlow.

Native oak and elm were the two most popular types of timber used for building before the seventeenth century. Oak was chosen for its strength, durability and weather and insect resistance, while elm was popular for its good working and bending properties, and its high water resistance. Unfortunately, thanks to the over-enthusiastic felling of these slow-growing trees, both species were in short supply by the late 1600s, and timber-rich houses gradually gave way to brick and stone construction.

Timber continued to be used in buildings over the next two centuries, but its presence was not as obvious. Roof timbers, joists, purlins – all these structural components were still made from timber, but it was often cheaper, less durable softwood, and these parts were hidden from view.

LEFT A glorious fourteenth-century timber-trussed roof at the Merchant Adventurers' Hall in York.

ABOVE RIGHT A carved wooden writhing snake from a door in the saloon at Uppark in West Sussex.

LEFT The tell-tale holes left by woodworm in panelling in the Long Gallery at Chastleton, Oxfordshire.

RIGHT Black and white timber in quatrefoil and chevron designs on Speke Hall, a sixteenth-century house in Merseyside.

Only in the attics of grand houses, or in the humble vernacular cottage, were exposed roof and wall timbers still a common feature.

Interiors of this period also incorporated wood, but in most cases doors, panelling, windows, skirting boards and cupboards were painted to disguise the natural material. These components were also made from the cheaper, more abundant softwoods, such as pine, which were considered too bland to be left unfinished. Only staircases, flooring and ornate doors and panelling were made from expensive hardwoods and designed to be left unpainted.

UNINVITED GUESTS

Seasoned timber can last for hundreds of years; you only have to see how long some of the country's wooden buildings have survived to know this is true. Damp conditions, however, make timber attractive to mould, fungus and wood-boring insects, such as woodworm and death-watch beetles: all these little blighters can cause significant damage if left untreated.

Wood-boring bugs

The two principal insects that cause damage to timber in the UK are the furniture beetle (*Anobium punctatum*), also commonly called 'woodworm', and the death-watch beetle (*Xestobium rufovillosum*). It can be difficult to tell which insect is attacking your timber, but here are some quick guidelines to help you identify and tackle these annoying bugs.

The best indicator is the size of the holes in your timber. Furniture beetles make small holes only 1 mm ($^1/_{32}$ in) across, whereas death-watch

From the largest beam to the smallest carving, timber is one of the most versatile building materials available to the house restorer.

beetle holes can be 3 mm ($^1/_8$ in) in diameter. Furniture beetles prefer softwoods to hardwoods, while death-watch beetles prefer hardwoods (especially oak). In general, both species will stay close under the surface of the timber in the sapwood (the soft part of the tree nearest the bark), but if the timber is wet for a prolonged period of time, or the infestation is very severe, both furniture beetles and death-watch beetles can attack the very centre of the timber, known as heartwood. Surface damage by wood-boring insects is rarely a serious problem, but if the heartwood is damaged, this affects the structural integrity of timber cut from it.

It can be tricky to establish whether an insect colony is active or not. If the activity has long since stopped, you need not do anything, but if you suspect the insects are still nibbling away, it's important to confirm this. With both the furniture beetle and the death-watch beetle look for fresh piles of wood dust (called 'frass') near the holes. You can also tell if the holes are being used by death-watch beetle by applying wax polish to the holes and waiting to see if they get reopened. The death-watch beetle also makes a characteristic tapping sound during late spring/early summer (this is the male beetle striking his head on a wooden surface to attract the female).

Timber treatments – If you suspect you have an active colony of furniture beetles or death-watch beetles, the first thing to do is to remove the source of dampness affecting the timber. Both species prefer wet wood, so reducing the moisture content of the timber should either decrease or totally stop the problem. The easiest way to do this is to stop any water coming into the house from either rising damp or penetrating damp, and

The Long Gallery at Little Moreton Hall, Cheshire. Wood panelling has been a favourite form of decoration and extra insulation since the mid-fifteenth century.

check for plumbing and guttering leaks. Second, remove any existing dampness with adequate heating and a dehumidifier (although do this slowly because drying out timber too quickly can cause it to crack). Make sure any paint finishes, plasters and renders are water permeable so that you're not trapping moisture in the fabric of the building. You should also check that any vents, airbricks and roof voids are clear: these often get blocked over time and cause water to become trapped.

In the past, timbers affected by insect attack were removed unnecessarily. In many cases, the damage was only superficial and wasn't affecting the structural integrity of the timber. This can be difficult to tell, however, so if you are in any doubt, you should contact a surveyor or structural engineer who can tell you how far the damage has spread. Choose an expert who is sympathetic to old buildings because he or she will be far less likely to advocate the unnecessary destruction of historic timbers. As a general rule, however, you should remove timber only if it is strictly necessary, and limit the amount to the absolute minimum.

Whether or not you use a timber treatment may depend on what your building society or bank has to say. Some mortgage lenders will demand that you get any sign of infestation, whether active or not, treated by a reputable company. Unfortunately, many 'treatments' are either destructive to the fabric of the building (as discussed above) or involve strong chemicals.

In the past it was common practice to spray highly toxic chemicals, such as DDT, dieldrin, pentachlorophenol, lindane, tributyl tin oxide and even arsenic, on the timber in our homes. Many of these chemicals have been linked to serious health problems, although that hasn't stopped some of

The timbers at Tan Farm Cottages, Essex, were so rotten that the concrete render was effectively holding the building up.

them being used even today. While modern chemical treatments, such as permethrin, organic zinc compounds, IPBC, dichlofluanid and propiconazole, are thought to be less toxic, concerns have still been raised about their health and environmental impact. One solution, which has come from the eco-building movement, is to use boron-based timber treatments.

Boron is a naturally occurring element, and inorganic compounds of it can be used to prevent or eradicate insect attack and fungal problems (including dry rot) in timber in a way that is both effective and safe. Most chemical treatments, whether sprayed or painted on, can reach only a few millimetres into the fabric of the timber. However, certain boron treatments, called glycol borates, can be absorbed up to 40 mm ($1\frac{1}{2}$ in) into the timber, allowing them to reach some of the most serious insect attacks. The Green Building Store has further information about boron-based timber treatments, but you could also ask a local contractor approved by the British Wood Preserving and Damp-proofing Association for advice (see page 246). Be aware, however, that each company will have its own favourite approach, some more environmentally or conservation-friendly than others. Do your research and get quotes from a few different companies if possible.

Rot

There are two types of rot you'll hear house restorers moan about: wet rot and dry rot. Both attack damp wood. The difference is that wet rot is a localized fungus (usually *Coniophora cerebella*, commonly called 'cellar fungus') and will affect only the area of timber that is wet. Dry rot, on the

A Shropshire timber-framed house.

other hand, is caused by a more aggressive fungus called *Serpula lachrymans*, which can spread from wet timber to dry timber, plaster and brickwork, causing significant damage along the way. Dry rot also prefers warmth and darkness, so you often find it behind panelling or under floorboards.

It can be difficult to tell whether you have wet rot or dry rot. Both types of rot darken wood and break down the surface of the timber into a cube pattern. Wet rot, however, sometimes produces a cobweb of dark fungal strands, while dry rot can develop into grey/white cotton wool-like sheets often covered with tiny orange spores. Dry rot also has a distinctive musty, mushroom-like smell.

In the initial stages of fungal decay wet rot and dry rot can look very similar, so it's important to seek specialist advice. As already mentioned, an unnecessarily heavy-handed approach to timber problems can result in

BATS AND THE LAW

In England, Scotland and Wales all bat species are protected under the Wildlife and Countryside Act 1981 and Conservation Regulations 1994. These make it illegal to intentionally kill, injure or capture bats, deliberately disturb bats, or damage, destroy or obstruct access to bat roosts. You will not be allowed to carry out any timber treatments on your property, especially in roof spaces, if it results in any of the above. If this problem affects you, contact the Bat Conservation Trust for more advice (see page 245).

LEFT Always use authentic finishes such as beeswax and linseed oil to preserve the look of old woodwork.

RIGHT Staircases are one of the few features likely to survive in their original condition in a historic house.

the destruction of precious ancient timbers. Equally, inadequate treatment of dry rot in particular can lead to disaster. Consult an independent professional who is familiar with timber rot in old buildings. Visit www.buildingconservation.com for a list of timber preservation trade bodies and consultants.

As with insect infestations, both wet and dry rot have sometimes been subject to over-the-top remedies in the past. The standard practice of removing 1 metre (3.3 ft) of sound timber surrounding an outbreak of dry rot has caused untold damage over the years. Newer research suggests that increasing ventilation and heating at the same time as removing sources of damp goes a long way to solving the problem. See pages 83–6 for advice about suitable timber treatments.

RESTORING WOODWORK

As well as being alert to the problems of rot and insect attack, it's also important to have a general understanding of how to repair and care for old timber. In any period property there will be numerous wooden structures, both fixed and freestanding, each of which will require gentle handling if they are going to last and look their best.

Below you'll find specific advice about the four most common timber structures in a historic house: staircases, panelling, doors and flooring. Windows have their own separate chapter in this book, but some general rules apply to all historic woodwork:

1 Never clean it if you don't have to: overenthusiastic scrubbing and stripping can get rid of years of beautiful patina and ruin the finish of a piece. Go easy with the sander too. The charm of old timber lies in its dents and scratches. Maker's names and tool marks are historical documents and need to be preserved.
2 Always try to use an authentic finish on timber: oils, waxes, gesso and traditional paints will look and perform better than modern varnishes and paints.
3 If you are dealing with important historic timbers, especially unique or valuable examples, don't try to restore them yourself – always seek professional advice.

Staircases

Staircase design varies enormously from house to house and era to era, from the grandest William and Mary staircases with ornate handcrafted newel posts and barley-sugar-twist balusters to Victorian mass-produced pine examples. One thing unites them all, however, and that is that they are among the features most likely to survive in a historic building. This is for two reasons: first, staircases are relatively expensive compared to other fittings in the home; second, they are a real pain to replace. That's great news for the would-be house restorer. The staircase is one of the most defining and noticeable features in a home, so if you've got the original, you're laughing.

Stairs consist of horizontal treads (the parts you step on), nosings (the overlapping lips) and risers (the vertical planks at the back of each step). The

railings (also called a balustrade) are made up of lots of individual balusters (tall, thin spindles) held together by the handrail. At the top and bottom of the staircase you'll find a newel post keeping the whole thing together.

If you've bought a property with the original timber staircase, the first thing you should do is try to conserve it if at all possible. Lots of things can go wrong with a wooden flight of stairs – from wobbly newel posts to broken balusters – but rarely is it necessary to replace the whole staircase. The basic design and construction of wooden staircases hasn't changed over the past three centuries, so a skilled joiner should be able to tackle even the most unpromising of jobs. Unless the problem is very minor (a squeaky tread, for example), it's best not to tackle fixing an antique staircase yourself, however; this is one job best left to the professionals. The same applies if you need any new pieces of staircase: use a trained wood-turner to make any missing balusters, or a woodcarver to replace missing ornamentation.

You can contribute, however, by ensuring that the work is in the correct style for the period. The joiner will be following instructions from you, so make sure you inform him or her of the correct design and detail for the staircase. Give them as much information as you can find out about the date of the stairs, wood type, construction and finish. Do as much research into the history of your staircase as possible. It might sound unimportant, but modern materials and historically inaccurate repairs can be disastrous for an old staircase, ruining the interior of the entire house. Conservation work on old staircases should be of the highest standard: joints should fit together snugly, traditional glues should be used (modern

Stick to professional carpenters and woodcarvers if you need to repair a staircase of historical interest, especially intricately carved sections such as newel posts, *above left*. This fine example, *right*, is from Thrumpton Hall, a Jacobean mansion in Nottinghamshire.

If you need to remove wood panelling for remedial work, ensure that you take great care and number each section.

adhesives are too strong), and, where possible, the original techniques and hand-tools should be employed.

Wood panelling

Lining the interior of a room with wood panelling has been all the rage since the second half of the fifteenth century. Not only does it serve a very practical purpose of keeping out the cold and covering up any unsightly walls, but it also serves a decorative purpose. Both hardwoods and softwoods were used for panelling from the word go, but only hardwood panelling was designed to be left in its natural state. Queen Anne panelling, for example, was often painted in muted, flat colours, green being a particular favourite, while Victorian Gothic panelling was executed mostly in bare oak. During the eighteenth century the fashion for wood panelling briefly faded, giving way to Rococo and Neoclassical plasterwork, but it didn't take long for the Victorians to revive the trend with their characteristic gusto.

As with timber staircases, it's vital to retain as much of your historic panelling as possible. Most repairs can be carried out *in situ*, but if it is necessary to remove any panels for conservation work, make sure it's done with extreme care. Wood panelling can be attached to the wall in any number of ways – huge nails, screws, pegs and fixing blocks – so take your time. Photograph each panel before you remove it, and make sure you number each one on the back so that you can reassemble them in the correct order.

Don't be tempted to strip back softwood panelling to reveal the natural wood underneath. Softwood was never intended to be left bare. Hardwood,

on the other hand, needs to be treated with wax polish: never use modern polyurethane varnishes on old wood. As with all antique timber, the less you intervene the better.

Doors

In a pre-1930s house you'll find one of two types of doors – battened or panelled. Battened doors are essentially planks nailed together, then braced across the back with horizontal pieces of wood called 'ledges'. This type of door has been in use since at least the Middle Ages, and remains a popular feature in rural properties up and down the country even today. The Arts and Crafts movement also loved the rustic simplicity of battened doors, but for the majority of Victorians panelled doors were seen as an eminently more sophisticated and elegant choice.

Panelled doors came into their own at the beginning of the eighteenth century. Before this time the complex carpentry needed to construct such doors made them too expensive for most householders. With the introduction of new, semi-automated technology, however, panelled doors could be made faster and cheaper than ever before. These doors also had the added benefit of using less wood than battened doors – a real bonus during a time when native hardwoods were growing scarcer by the day.

As with staircases, the wrong type of door can ruin the interior of a historic building. In general, Georgian doors have six panels, and Victorian doors have four. However, there is such a variety of designs and finishes that it's worth reading up about the exact type of door for your

LEFT Fine examples of old doors – a typical battened door, and two early panelled doors.

RIGHT First impressions – the front door is always the most impressive and expensive in the entire house.

house. The Victorian Society (see page 250) has a very useful guide to choosing the right door for your property.

Of course, you might find more than one type of door in a house. In Georgian houses, for example, it's not uncommon to find that the interior doors on the ground floor (the most public space) are made from expensive hardwood, while the upper storeys will have cheaper painted softwood examples. With this in mind, it's worth thinking twice about having stripped softwood doors in a historic house. It might be the current trend, but it pays scant attention to historical accuracy. It's also worth knowing that the process of chemically dipping a door can weaken the joints and compromise its stability. If you do need to remove old paint from a door, you can brush on a topical application of stripper, which is then scraped off. Heat guns tend to burn the wood and are best avoided. Also, don't be tempted to sand off old layers of paint: pre-1950s paint often contained lead, which is harmful if you breathe it in or swallow it. The Department for Environment's website (see page 246) has more information on dealing with old lead paint.

For more detailed information about mending wooden doors, check out the technical advice at SPAB's website (see page 249).

Flooring

As with all the other hardwood timber in historic houses, that used for flooring was designed to be seen: cheaper softwoods, on the other hand, were often disguised to resemble something else. Before the eighteenth century, when native hardwoods were still plentiful, oak was commonly

used as a flooring material in even the most humble of houses. After this date, however, oak became too expensive for many householders, and its use was often restricted to public areas of the house designed to impress visitors, such as the receptions rooms.

When softwoods were used they often received some kind of finish. Limewash was popular and produced an attractive, silvery-white sheen. A similar effect was produced by scrubbing floors with dry sand. Softwood floors might also be stained to resemble hardwood, treated with oil-based paint (although this was more common in the USA), stencilled or covered up with large rugs, floorcloths or carpets.

LEFT Heavy wood is used in the panelling, flooring and ceiling in the Great Hall at Blackwell, Bowness-on-Windermere, one of Britain's most important Arts and Crafts houses.

RIGHT An unrestored section of parquet floor from Ham House in Surrey.

By the early nineteenth century parquetry (hardwood veneers laid in patterns) had became fashionable, although many houses used it simply as a border around a carpeted floor. Not until the Victorian era did entire floors of parquetry and marquetry (wood inlays) become common.

Floor treatments – If you want bare floorboards – whether hardwood or softwood – the best finish is floor wax. Never use linseed oil, as it attracts dirt and will darken over time. Also avoid polyurethane varnishes, as they scratch easily and tend to yellow with age.

To remove general stains from wood floors, use a gentle solution of glycerine and water (very fine steel wool may be employed for some of the more stubborn stains). Greasy stains are best removed with kitchen soap with a good lye content – the old-fashioned traditional soap brands are best for this, such as Savon de Marseille. If the floor has a wax finish, be sure to rewax the area after cleaning it. Water marks, which lighten a floor, may need to be stained, then rewaxed. A wide variety of proprietary floor treatments are available, so shop around for conservation-approved brands.

If you need to repair a section of old flooring, consider two important points. The first is to consult a skilled joiner, who will be knowledgeable in historic timber floor construction and be able to make an invisible repair; the second is to use reclaimed timber that matches the original floor in colour, age and patina. Salvage yards often have a good selection of reclaimed floorboards, joists and parquetry. Sometimes they even have entire floors in stock, so if a room is completely devoid of a floor covering, this can be a quick way to achieve great results while keeping a historically accurate feel to the building.

LEFT The use of glass became more widespread during the Tudor period.

RIGHT The cruck house shows the ingenuity of Elizabethan craftsmen. A curved tree makes a curved truss!

TUDOR STYLE (1500–1600)

In the previous chapter we looked at the medieval peasant's house, the epitome of simple design and humble materials. In direct contrast, the Tudor country house represents architectural extravagance on a scale previously unimagined and rarely matched even today.

The English country house didn't really exist before the reign of Henry VIII. Prior to that time, the medieval manor houses of the wealthy were primarily functional buildings, the owner achieving status through worthy actions rather than via the magnificence of his home. All this changed with the Dissolution of the Monasteries between 1536 and 1540, when Henry VIII redistributed the Church's vast wealth and land among his loyal supporters. Rich beyond their wildest dreams and keen to be accepted as the ruling class, the new elite set about building large, extravagant houses. As William Harrison pointed out in his book *Description of England* (1577), 'Each one desireth to set his house aloft on the hill, to be seen afar off, and cast forth his beams of stately and curious workmanship into every quarter of the country.'

Courtiers often went well beyond their means, almost bankrupting themselves to create houses grand enough to accommodate the monarch on his or her 'Royal Progress', a stately tour around the country during the summer months. In 1535, for example, Nicholas Poyntz built a magnificent new east wing on his moated manor house, Acton Court, in readiness for the arrival of Henry VIII and his second wife, Anne Boleyn. This generous gesture didn't go unnoticed, and Poyntz was duly knighted during the royal visit.

But these new stately piles weren't just larger versions of the medieval manor house. Things had changed. The Tudor period was one of greater political and social stability than in previous centuries. Large houses in medieval times were often heavily fortified, the need for defence creating inward-looking buildings grouped around a courtyard. During Tudor times, by contrast, houses of the wealthy started to become outward-looking, turning away from fortifications and focusing instead on exterior ornament and 'showing off'.

Wealth was demonstrated by the extensive use of glass, still a hugely expensive luxury at the time. A fine example of this is Hardwick Hall in Derbyshire. Built in the 1590s, the house walls are pierced with enormous mullioned windows, giving rise to the famous contemporary couplet 'Hardwick Hall, more glass than wall'. Bricks were another 'must-have' building material of the day. Handmade, expensive and smaller than modern bricks, only the richest households could afford this relatively new building material (the art of brick-making had all but disappeared during the Middle Ages in England). A dazzling example of Tudor brickwork can be seen in Surrey at Hampton Court Palace, the great house started by Cardinal Wolsey and given to Henry VIII in 1525 in a desperate attempt to curry the king's favour.

But it wasn't just new materials that were making an entrance. New ideas were also influencing the great house-builders of the day. Renaissance motifs, symmetry and balance became highly desirable – at Lacock Abbey in Wiltshire, for example, Sir William Sharington converted the thirteenth-century abbey into a family home in 1539, building a polygonal tower topped with a balustrade in the classical style. Despite this, few Tudor houses totally embraced the ideas from the Renaissance. Classical ideas, craftsmen and pattern books were filtering through to England from the Continent, but in the latter part of the Tudor period Queen Elizabeth's volatile relationship with Catholic Europe sometimes made the

LEFT Hardwick Hall is a good example of the bombastic, self-assured houses the Elizabethan court produced.

RIGHT Anne Hathaway's cottage, near Stratford, with its typical Tudor thatch, timber frame and cottage garden.

exchange difficult. As a result, country houses from this time often have a wonderfully eclectic mix of medieval Gothic and new Renaissance features. (For more about Gothic architecture, see pages 148–151.)

Longleat, one of the finest country houses of the period and viewed by many as a high point in Tudor architecture, is a fine example of eclecticism. Started in 1554 and taking twenty years to reach completion, the building is a fascinating mix of Renaissance influences and the native Gothic. The stone-mullioned bay windows are a direct descendant of the Gothic style, yet the house is also decorated with pilasters and busts of Roman emperors, both details lifted straight from classical architecture.

At the opposite end of the social scale, one of the best examples of a typical Tudor town house is Shakespeare's birthplace in Henley Street, Stratford-upon-Avon. Since 1847 the house has been owned and protected by a trust that has stopped it being altered or updated, thus preserving it as a fascinating and authentic glimpse into Elizabethan life. Painstakingly restored, this simple half-timbered property was originally built to a rectangular plan, containing just a parlour, an adjoining hall and a workshop downstairs (Shakespeare's father was a glove-maker and wool dealer). On the first floor there are three rooms, used for either sleeping or storage. Seven members of the Shakespeare family would have lived in this small house, along with a handful of servants and possibly an apprentice to the glove-making business. A huge open hearth dominates the hall, while the walls are plastered around exposed timber beams. The furniture is simple, stout and wooden. The walls are adorned with brightly painted wall cloths, while the four-poster bed in one bedroom comes complete with a truckle bed that stows away underneath, and beautiful woollen drapes.

The fact that you can visit Shakespeare's birthplace and many of the other Tudor buildings mentioned earlier makes life much easier for the would-be house restorer. Books and magazine articles are all well and good, but there can be little substitute for going to see the real thing. Few people reading these words will be restoring a Tudor house from scratch, but a surprising number of houses still have Tudor features or remnants of their original sixteenth-century layout. Understanding and preserving these ever-diminishing fragments of history is what good restoration is all about.

STONEWORK

Stonework is everywhere. You find it used in almost every part of an historic building – foundations, walls, lintels, roof tiles, window sills, steps and decorative carvings – but contrary to what you might expect, it's also one of the most easily damaged materials. Damp, frost, poor repairs and general weathering can all take their toll, so it's important to have a basic understanding of how to care for old stone.

Building stone comes in two basic forms. Ashlar stone is quarried, squared and neatly dressed into perfectly shaped blocks. The blocks are cut so precisely that they need very little mortar between them, and provide an elegant, although expensive, building material. You'll often see this kind of stone used in public buildings and town houses for the well-to-do.

Rubble stone is less expensive than ashlar. 'Free rubble' consists of rough stones that are uneven in shape and often used as found. Although it is quarried like ashlar stone, free rubble was just as often picked straight off the fields and made into farm buildings and peasants' cottages. While rubble stone was also used on smarter houses, it was neatly squared off for a smarter, more uniform finish. This is called 'dressed rubble'.

From huge theatrical statements, such as the Royal Crescent in Bath, *left*, to minute carved details, *above right*, stonework is omnipresent in British architecture.

A house can have both ashlar stone and rubble elements used together: for example, ashlar may be used as a facing on a rough rubble wall. Historically, ashlar tended to be an up-market stone, and was often traded around the country via waterways. Rubble stone is a humbler material and usually came from the local area, either from quarries or land cleared by farmers. It was often chosen for its availability rather than its durability.

GEOLOGY MADE SIMPLE

Understanding the geology and behaviour of different types of stone helps house restorers to predict and remedy many common problems. Learning that sandstone is damaged by acid, for example, helps us to understand the problems caused by acid rain and stops us from using acid-based cleaners in any maintenance work.

In simple terms, there are three main types of stone: igneous, sedimentary and metamorphic.

ABOVE, LEFT TO RIGHT Carstone, flint and blue lias – just three examples of the different types of stone native to the UK.

RIGHT Ashlar stone – elegant, expensive and a favourite with Georgian architects.

Igneous stone

As its name might suggest, this type of rock is created by fire, specifically the fiery lava or magma produced by volcanoes. Among the many forms of igneous rock, which include basalt, gabbro and tuff, granite is the best-known example.

Granite – is hard-wearing, durable and frost resistant, and these qualities have made it a popular choice for the exterior cladding of historic buildings, paving, high-traffic flooring and kitchen worktops. For carving, granite is best used for large, simple shapes, as fine detail is difficult to achieve on such a hard material.

Sedimentary stone

This type of rock is produced when clay, sand or gravel is carried by wind or water and deposited on the surface of the land. Over time, this sediment

consolidates into stone. Limestone and sandstone are the two best-known examples used in historic structures.

Limestones – are formed from sediment laid down in sea water or fresh water, and contain calcite, a mineral made from the crushed shells and bones of sea creatures. Calcite is dissolved by acid, hence the tendency of limestone to be damaged by acid rain. Limestones are softer than granite and therefore easier to shape into rectangular blocks or carve in fine detail. You've probably heard of the three most famous types: Cotswold limestone, white Portland and yellowy Bath stone. Limestone is also the raw material for quicklime and lime putty (see 'Lime' chapter).

Sandstone – is made from consolidated sand, and varies in durability, depending on its composition. Siliceous sandstone, which contains a high proportion of the mineral silica, is very hard and strong. Argillaceous sandstone, on the other hand, contains a high percentage of clay, which makes for a much less durable stone. Like limestone, sandstone is relatively easy to work with, making it a popular choice as a building material. Well-known sandstones include millstone grit from West Yorkshire, Darley Dale sandstone from Derbyshire, York stone and the red sandstones of Cheshire.

Flint – is widely used in British buildings, especially in areas of the southeast and East Anglia, because it is extremely tough in composition. The Georgians often used it in conjunction with brick or stone to add

A detail from the impressive fireplace in the Marble Hall at Clandon Park, Surrey.

decorative interest, extra strength and stability to their structures, but it has actually been used as a building material since well before Roman times. The fact that flint is easily collected from places such as beaches and riverbeds has probably been a large contributory factor to its widespread use.

Metamorphic stone

These are rocks that have gone through a process of transformation caused by either intense heat or immense pressure. Both igneous and sedimentary rocks can be changed into metamorphic rocks, and some of the best known are marble (which is metamorphosed limestone) and slate (metamorphosed mudstone).

Marble – is one of the most expensive stones used in building, and is often reserved for decoration, floors and fireplaces. The most famous type is pure white Carrara marble, which comes from Italy, but marble is also available in lots of different patterns and colours – pinks, greens, browns. Although marble lends itself to elaborate carving, it is porous and therefore easy to stain. It's also easily damaged by acid, and does not weather well if used outdoors in the UK. Sometimes conservationists and architects refer to certain types of stone as 'marble' when they are not marble at all. These are often simply stones that have been cut and highly polished, and include Purbeck marble (which is actually a limestone) and white alabaster.

ABOVE The devil's in the detail – look out for unusual pieces of stone carving such as dragons, gargoyles and floral motifs.

LEFT Welsh slate is easily split into thin sheets, making it ideal for roof tiles.

Slate – is another metamorphic rock, mostly grey, green or blueish-purple in colour. Welsh slate is probably the best-known variety. It's easy to split into flat, smooth plates, which makes it ideal for roof tiles, but it was also frequently used for fireplace surrounds and kitchen floors during the nineteenth century. Thick slabs of slate were also used for steps, cisterns and larder shelves.

Artificial stone

We tend to think of manufactured stone as a modern invention, but stone substitutes have been available since the eighteenth century. Made from a mixture of sand, cement, aggregate and water, artificial stone was a cheap alternative to the real thing and often replaced it in both exterior and interior contexts. It was also cast into decorative shapes to resemble stone carvings.

Although cheaper than natural stone, artificial stone poses its own particular problems. If it splits or weathers, its rough aggregate centre (rather like the centre of a Toffee Crisp chocolate bar) will be revealed. If artificial stone contains calcite-rich aggregates, such as limestone or marble, it will also be damaged by acid.

Coade stone – is one of the most famous examples of artificial stone, but, unlike other types, it was fired to yield a highly durable ceramic material. Produced by Eleanor Coade at the Artificial Stone Factory in south London from 1769, this highly popular and versatile material could be modelled into crisp shapes, and was used as a stone substitute for external decoration, especially for sculpture, monuments and architectural details,

LEFT Even in brick buildings stone was used for key features, like this one at Grafham House in Surrey.

RIGHT Stone might seem a tough and durable material but it can be easily damaged by water, over-zealous cleaning and exposure to the elements.

such as keystones and plaques. It became a favourite with renowned architects of the day, including Robert Adam, John Nash and Sir John Soane, and some of London's most famous buildings, such as Buckingham Palace, include Coade stone details. Unfortunately, the Coade factory closed shortly after Eleanor's death in 1821, and the material fell out of use over the next thirty years.

CLEANING STONEWORK

In general, it's best not to clean stonework unless you really have to. Stone buildings develop a gentle patina over time, and overcleaning can result in them looking too new. There's also a real danger that the stone will be damaged in the process.

However, there are some types of grime that it *is* advisable to remove. Bird droppings, which are acidic, can be especially harmful to limestone. Salt can also be very destructive, particularly on buildings and walls next to roads that are salted during wintertime. If you want to get rid of surface grime, droppings or mould, the gentlest approach is always best. Most dirt will come off with just a light scrub, using a soft-bristled brush and water. Avoid saturating the stonework, however, and never clean stone with water when there is a risk of frost. If water fails to shift the stains, you may need a chemical cleaning solution, but choose a non-acidic variety if it's being used on limestone or marble. The same rules apply for stone statuary and carving. Scrubbing should not be employed if the surface of the stone is fragile or crumbling.

Certain stones are so soft they can be easily marked, as with these two interesting examples of ancient graffiti – at Carlisle Castle, *left*, and Holy Trinity Church in West Hendred, Oxfordshire, *above right*.

If your restoration project has been abandoned for some time, it may have suffered from vandalism. Graffiti is notoriously difficult to remove, and will need more than soap and elbow grease. Very abrasive forms of cleaning, such as sandblasting or gritblasting, however, will damage soft surfaces, such as sandstone, limestone and artificial stone, so should be avoided at all costs. They can lead to accelerated weathering by pitting the surface of the stone, allowing moisture and decay to do their worst.

Even water can be abrasive if applied under very high pressure. Look into specialist micro-abrasive cleaning techniques, laser cleaning, and new technologies, such as the Farrow System (a gentle cleaning system that uses volcanic sand, heated water and low-pressurized air), which aim to remove any unwanted finishes while leaving the stone completely undamaged. A conservation body, such as English Heritage or SPAB (see pages 247 and 249), may be able to advise you about the best course of action.

It's better not to remove old layers of limewash and traditional distemper paints from stone, but if an inappropriate modern paint has been applied and is trapping in moisture, you can remove it using a paint stripper specially formulated for use on stone. HomeStrip™ by Eco Solutions is an environmentally friendly paint stripper that can be used on brick, marble and concrete, and even on very soft porous stone.

To clean slate, use a soft brush and gentle washing-up liquid. Wipe off any excess liquid immediately and use a dry cloth to finish. If you want to seal the slate on your fireplace, use linseed oil, but not in areas that get very hot.

Marble needs extra special attention, and you should always do a patch test first. Wash with a solution of warm water and gentle detergent or a mild neutral-pH cleanser specifically developed for stone surfaces. High-alkaline or mild acidic cleaners can dull, stain or even damage the finish. Buff dry with a clean cloth. Stubborn stains on marble will require 'poulticing'. You can either make your own poultice (see below) or buy a ready-made paste, such as Sepiolite. Apply to the stain and leave to dry. As the poultice dries, it draws out the stain. Restoration experts Bricks and Brass (see page 245) recommend the following recipes to remove stains from marble:

For soot stains, mix together untreated flour, baking powder and distilled water to form a thick, creamy paste. Apply the paste 1 cm (½ in) thick to the stain and cover with plastic to form an airtight seal. Leave for 48 hours, then remove the paste, rinse with water and buff dry. Reapply a second time if needed. For oily stains, follow the soot stain recipe, but replace the baking powder and distilled water with white spirit.

REPOINTING STONEWORK

There are two key factors to consider when repointing old stonework. The first is to use a mortar that is similar in composition and colour to the original material. If your building pre-dates 1850, this will usually mean a lime mortar, either non-hydraulic or feebly to moderately hydraulic, depending on the situation (see 'Lime' chapter). Use a cement mortar and chances are you'll cause decay of the stonework, and the colour of the mortar will be wrong for the building.

ABOVE The stone tower at Biddulph in Staffordshire was badly dilapidated.

ABOVE RIGHT A wonderful naive carved face at Biddulph.

The second consideration is what style of pointing to use. It's best to call in the experts at this stage, but if you're skilled enough to have a go, remember to avoid unsightly modern practices, such as ribbon pointing. This not only looks anachronistic, but also sticks out further than the stonework, thus providing a ledge for water to collect on. Any water that sits on the pointing will seep into the stonework and cause problems in the future.

Some historic properties have walls that were built without using mortar at all. This technique, known as drystone walling, is used mainly for field boundaries, but there are examples of it used for single-storey dwellings. If no mortar was used in the construction of your period building, leave it that way. The recent revival in the art of drystone walling now means that there are experts up and down the country whom you can consult about such matters.

REPAINTING STONEWORK

As discussed in the 'Lime' chapter, many old buildings were designed to be limewashed. If this applies to your building, keep up the tradition. Not only will it make your historic property look more authentic, but it will actually help to preserve the exterior of the building. Certain modern waterproof or water-repelling coatings can trap moisture and lead to the crumbling of the stone surface. Consult a stone restoration expert before you apply any finish of this kind.

Unfortunately an angle grinder caused significant damage to the stonework at Higher Hill Farm, Lancashire. Chipping out should really be done by hand.

REPAIRING STONEWORK

What causes stone to fail in the first place? There are three main culprits:

- Weathering
- Water
- Bad repairs

The first you can do very little about. From the moment it is quarried, stone naturally decays over time, especially if exposed to severe weather or pollution. Surfaces will lose their smoothness, and carvings their detail. Many of the lovely limestone colleges in Oxford, for example, have been damaged by the build-up of traffic fumes. Lime renders and limewash can help reduce the impact of weathering, but these finishes might not be appropriate for your type of building. Find out whether your stonework was designed to be exposed to the weather; if not, cover it with limewash or lime render again. Failing that, you have two other choices: do nothing (if the damage isn't affecting the integrity of the building, this approach is often the best), or get it repaired.

Water damage you *can* do something about. Poor maintenance of guttering, roofs and downpipes causes leaks, which in turn damage stonework. Keep an eye out for cracked pipes, rampant ivy, guttering blocked with leaves and missing roof tiles. A few minutes a week spent maintaining a property will save you a fortune in stone repairs in the future. Water also affects certain types of structure more than others,

especially if they have architectural details where water tends to collect, such as copings, cornices and other projecting courses.

Bad workmanship and inappropriate repairs are also to blame for problems in historic stonework. As explained in the 'Lime' chapter, cement mortar and render can damage stone walls, either by causing the stone to crack, or by trapping moisture next to the wall. The same applies to modern masonry paints, which may also be causing damage. If possible, remove the inappropriate material and refinish with a lime-based product.

It's also worth mentioning that inherent structural problems, such as subsidence, can damage stonework. If you think this applies to your restoration project, you'll have to tackle the underlying causes of the problem before you even think about repairing the stone. Check with your surveyor, who will help you decide the best way to stabilize the building.

Typical repairs

Sometimes you can't avoid making repairs to stonework. In general, it's best to employ a master stonemason, especially on finely carved work or ashlar stone. The Conservation Register (see page 246) has a list of trained stonemasons to choose from, but even if you employ someone to do the work, it's still a good idea to know the basic types of repairs.

Cracking – A common problem in stonework, cracking is often caused by minor movement or water penetration. Fine cracks can be filled with an epoxy-based filler, while larger cracks can be filled with lime grout. Very significant cracks may need to be pinned.

Matching new stone to old. In a few years these dramatic repairs will have gently weathered to fit in with the existing stone.

Rusting ironwork – It is common to see iron railings, gates, pins, rings, anchors and so forth embedded in stone walls, but when they begin to rust at the base, they expand, causing the surrounding stone to split. The rust can also stain the stonework. If ironwork is corroding, it will need to be removed or replaced to prevent further damage. A new metal substitute should be used, preferably one that is non-corroding, such as stainless steel.

Decay – Stones can spall (splinter), flake and crumble away over time. This commonly arises because they have been laid the wrong way. As sedimentary rocks, limestones and sandstones have naturally occurring layers called 'bedding planes' (imagine slices of bread stacked on top of each other to make a loaf). It's vital that a stone with bedding planes is laid in the right way – usually with the planes running horizontally rather than vertically – otherwise large pieces or sheets of the stone will simply separate and fall off over time.

How much you interfere with decay and attempt to restore your stonework will depend on a number of factors, not least whether your building is listed, the cost implications and whether the damaged stonework is structurally unsound or letting in water. With rubble-stone walls, it's usually necessary to replace or repair a stone only if it is so badly decayed that it stops being structurally safe (i.e. it can't support what's above it), or it allows water to become trapped inside the wall. When this happens you have two choices: either replace the stone with a matching one, or perform what's known as a 'plastic repair'.

LEFT The slate at Heolas Fawr in Wales was very poor quality, and years of tough coastal weather had stripped the stonework of limewash and grout.

RIGHT Many of the finest Cotswold cottages have survived due to a lack of intervention rather than over-zealous renovation.

If you decide to replace the stone, it's vital to source the right type. Mixing limestone and sandstone rocks together, for example, results in the decay of the sandstone because magnesium or calcium sulphates leach out of the limestone and attack the sandstone. To source the appropriate stone, check out local reclamation yards and quarries. The quarry where your stone originally came from may have closed, but conservation builders and master stonemasons in your area will have a good idea of compatible supplies near by.

If you don't want to replace the stone, you can always perform a plastic repair. In much the same way that a dentist drills a tooth before inserting a filling, a mason making a plastic repair will cut away the decayed stone back to solid stone, then fill the void with a carefully selected mixture of lime, sand and crushed stone. Natural pigments are sometimes added to help the repair match the original stonework.

In the same way that lime mortar should be weaker than the brick it surrounds, so plastic repairs should be slightly weaker than the surrounding stone. This makes the repair the 'sacrificial element' in any expansion and contraction of the stone, rather than the repair causing the stone to crack. Plastic repairs require great skill to get them right, and should be attempted only by a professional restorer.

Plastic repairs are also carried out on ashlar stone, but in general they work best on rubble walls and in small areas, such as mouldings and carvings. Severely damaged ashlar stones may need what's known as a 'Dutchman repair' instead. Again, the decayed part of the stone is cut away by the mason, but this time a new piece of stone is cut to fit and slotted

into the hole. The biggest challenge here, as with any stone repairs, is finding a suitable matching replacement.

With all these repairs, it's best to do the absolute minimum possible. Replacing or cutting away damaged stone is an essentially destructive process and should be viewed as a last resort.

REBUILDING STONEWORK

Only in extreme cases, such as acute instability, is it advisable to take down and rebuild a stone building. If you are forced to rebuild, it's important to take photographs and make drawings while numbering and recording the position of each stone so that the building can be successfully restored to its original appearance. You can temporarily number the stones using chalk, but you'll also need to number them permanently on a face that will be hidden, using exterior paint and a fine artist's brush. While dismantling the stones, take careful note of the thickness and composition of the mortar, the pointing details and any other quirks of the building.

LEFT The terrace was a new idea that transformed Georgian cities.

RIGHT Lindsey House in London was a revolutionary design, which helped define the Palladian style.

THE GEORGIAN CITY (1714–1837)

When George I acceded to the throne in 1714, British cities were still small, rambling and essentially medieval in layout. By the time the Georgian era came to an end in 1830, however, the country's urban centres had become dominated by grand, classically inspired terraces and squares. This radical evolution was primarily due to the emergence of developers – men who built thousands of private houses in great schemes, such as London's Regents Park and the Royal Crescent in Bath. It was through commerce, as opposed to ideologically driven state intervention, that the Georgian city was born.

The classical architecture of Renaissance Italy reached its full height in the early fifteenth century. This new style, which raided the design ideas of ancient Rome, travelled throughout Europe, influencing and changing local styles. However, it wasn't until the early seventeenth century and the great architect Inigo Jones that a British classical style began to evolve. Through a series of buildings at the turn of the seventeenth century, Jones developed the basic proportions and details that came to dominate Georgian architecture a century later. Known as the 'Palladian' style after Andrea Palladio, a sixteenth-century Italian architect whose work deeply influenced Jones, it was a simple, pared-down form of classicism, of which the Queen's House in Greenwich is a fine example. This building was revolutionary at the time, and still stands gracefully behind Greenwich Hospital to create one of the finest architectural compositions of its time. In 1640 a less regal but equally significant row of houses was built at Lincoln's Inn Fields in London by William Newton. Not only did the project embody the Palladian principles, but it was part of a terrace built by a developer for an urban square.

The Lincoln's Inn Fields development encapsulated all the components that would define the Georgian cityscape: a classical style, the terrace, the square and the backing of private developers. However, it took nearly 100 years for these factors to combine again. Housing development in Britain was seriously interrupted by the Civil War and Great Fire of London, both in the middle of the seventeenth century. The Palladian style did not become

widely accepted until the 1720s, when the development of Grosvenor Square in London provided the next big evolutionary step.

Along the same lines as Lincoln's Inn Fields, the Grosvenor development was conceived as a formal square by the landowner, then divided up and sold to different developers. The plot on the eastern side was bought by John Simmonds, who built seven houses in a terrace. But instead of treating them as seven different buildings, he made them look like a single palatial block. The centre house had a triangular pediment on the roof, and the end houses were emphasized so that the overall appearance of the terrace was far more impressive than the individual parts. Built for upwardly mobile merchants, it fulfilled the Georgian desire to show off new-found wealth. The idea also had political appeal, representing grand urban planning created by commerce. In France, Britain's great rival, this kind of development occurred only with the blessing of the state and autocratic king, Louis XV. Grosvenor Square was seen as a blow for the democratic over the despotic, a product of market forces and 'freemen'.

The next big step for the Georgian city didn't actually happen in a city, but in the relatively small town of Bath. By the 1720s this wool town had become renowned for the properties of its natural springs, which had attracted the Romans over 1500 years earlier. Now it drew royal health-seekers, and with them the rich hangers-on from London society. This migratory population brought with it a huge influx of money and a need for new housing to match the status of its new visitors. That need was answered most notably by John Wood the elder and his son, John Wood the younger, who over a period of forty years revolutionized both the Bath townscape and urban planning in general.

While Wood the elder was living in London, he approached landowners in Bath with a scheme for a row of houses heavily influenced by developments he'd seen in the capital, particularly in Grosvenor Square. The landowners of Bath responded well to his plans, and in 1729 he moved to Bath to begin building Queen Square. The square itself was a highly accomplished piece of design, but more importantly it set the tone for the revolutionary designs that followed. Wood's ambition was to imbue Bath with the character of its former Roman occupants. He didn't live to see the discovery of the original Roman baths, but had studied classics and knew of Bath's Roman history. His vision was for a forum, a circus and what he called an 'imperial gymnasium', which, although a far-fetched dream,

manifested itself in a series of extraordinary developments. The circus, begun by Wood the elder in 1754, was originally conceived as a place for sports exhibitions, but ended up as a variation on the residential square. A highly decorative row of terrace houses was curved into a circle with a garden in the middle.

Wood the elder died before the circus was finished, so it was left to his son to complete. Having achieved this, Wood the younger went on to conceive the Royal Crescent. This took the idea of the circus and opened it out to form half an ellipse. Using giant ionic columns on the front of the buildings, he created a sense of scale and grandeur that far exceeded anything seen before. The Royal Crescent was an instant success and copied throughout the country, becoming a mainstay of Georgian city planning.

ABOVE The Circus in Bath.
BELOW Inigo Jones's Queen's House in Greenwich.

WINDOWS AND GLASS

Conservation experts will tell you that no other architectural element has the potential to enhance or ruin a house as much as a window. Feelings run high among restorers. Hugh Lander, author of *The House Restorer's Guide*, gushes:

> '[Windows] spell out rhythms like passages of music. In one façade they are staccato, like the exclamations in an operatic recitative. They may march across the face of a building in a lively manner, like the allegro movement of a symphony or they may adopt a cool, reflective disposition which might be described as andante. The composition can express itself in beguiling twin minuets of white double-hung sashes enclosing a central Venetian window, like one of those elegant Haydn trios which can haunt you for the whole of a summer afternoon.'

Windows undoubtedly play a crucial role in the aesthetic harmony of the home. They've also been described as the 'eyes' of a house. They give the building focus and proportion, and provide a central point for our attention. The right windows can bring a building to life. The wrong windows will utterly destroy the visual and historical feel of a property. That's why, if you're restoring a house, it's important to choose your windows with the utmost care.

LEFT Historic glazing, like this stained-glass panel from Stoneacre in Kent, has an inherent richness and sparkle that is difficult to replicate.

ABOVE RIGHT At Higher Hill Farm in Lancashire, getting double glazing into stone-mullioned windows took considerable skill and ingenuity.

UPVC? DON'T EVEN THINK ABOUT IT

Before we go any further it's important to say one thing. Forget uPVC. In recent years there has been a trend to fit plastic windows into all sorts of historic buildings. Don't do it – ever.

Dramatic Gothic-style full-height windows at Longner Hall in Shropshire.

Around £2 billion is spent each year in Britain ripping out old windows and replacing them with plastic frames. People put in uPVC windows thinking that they are cheaper to buy and maintain. This isn't necessarily true. English Heritage believes that it's actually cheaper to maintain and repair historic timber windows than to replace them with plastic. Properly constructed and treated wooden frames can last for years if cared for (hence the survival of wooden window frames in many of the country's oldest buildings), while uPVC can need replacing after as little as twenty years. Plastic window frames also warp and discolour with age. With wooden windows, you simply repaint or patch the frame when it starts to show signs of ageing.

The designs of uPVC windows are also totally at odds with historic authenticity. Companies may offer 'Georgian-style' or 'Tudor-style' windows, but these are simply crude pastiches of the genuine article, often mixing styles from different eras. Just as the details and styling are inaccurate, so the materials are inauthentic. Furthermore, if you're bothered about the environment, uPVC windows are made from a non-renewable resource, and are thought to have a negative effect on the environment. Greenpeace notes that six of the fifteen most serious industrial pollutants are used in the manufacture of uPVC.

On a financial note, installing uPVC windows in a historic building will knock significant amounts of money off the value of the property. Channel Five recently asked interior designers Justin Ryan and Colin McAllister to investigate the twenty quickest ways to lose money on your property. Unsurprisingly, uPVC windows came out high on the list: 'uPVC

LEFT Charles Rennie Mackintosh designed the windows to be a central feature in his House for an Art Lover in Glasgow.

RIGHT A beautiful example of Arts and Crafts stained glass from Blackwell, Bowness-on-Windermere.

screams cheap and particularly off-putting in period housing. The worst offender is uPVC windows with a lead criss-cross or diamond pattern.' TV property expert Naomi Cleaver agrees: 'uPVC will cost you dear. Taste might be subjective, but it still has a price... The majority of buyers find uPVC windows a turn-off, and typically, when making an offer on a property with uPVC windows, will reduce it by several thousand pounds.' She sums up the whole argument perfectly: 'Putting uPVC windows in a period property is like making your grandmother wear a shell suit.'

Fortunately, people who own listed buildings will find it hard to get planning permission to install uPVC windows. According to English Heritage, the Secretary of State has dismissed over 90 per cent of appeals against the refusal of Listed Building Consent for replacing traditional single-glazed sash windows with double-glazed uPVC windows because the new windows would detrimentally affect the special character and appearance of the building. Despite this reassuring statistic, it still doesn't bear thinking about all the thousands of historic unlisted buildings that may end up getting a uPVC make-over from hell.

BUILDING REGULATIONS AND HISTORIC WINDOWS

One of the confusing factors in this whole uPVC debate has been the new Building Regulations that came into force in April 2002. The government, keen to tackle global warming and energy efficiency, has set strict standards for improving heat loss in the home, particularly through windows. Double glazing, one of the benefits of uPVC windows, is the obvious answer to heat loss, but most modern windows look out of place in a period property. On the other hand, few historic windows meet the levels recommended for conserving heat. The result is a complex problem: how to balance the need for energy conservation with the special interest and appearance of historic buildings?

People are often too hasty to replace old window frames, iron catches and glass panes. Preserve what you can of the original structure of your house.

Part L of the new Building Regulations clearly states:

> 'The need to conserve the special characteristics of ... historic buildings needs to be recognized... The aim should be to improve energy efficiency where and to the extent that it is practically possible, always provided that the work does not prejudice the character of the historic building, or increase the risk of long-term deterioration to the building fabric or fittings. In arriving at an appropriate balance between historic building conservation and energy conservation, it would be appropriate to take into account the advice of the local planning authority's conservation officer.'

So there you have it. Get advice straight from the horse's mouth. Your local conservation officer should be fully clued up about the latest recommendations for historic windows, replacements and energy efficiency. On top of this it's a good idea to do your own homework and get a copy of English Heritage's very useful leaflet 'Balancing the Needs for Energy Conservation with Those of Building Conservation: An Interim Guidance Note on the Application of Part L'. You can download it from their website or telephone for more information (see page 247).

In the meantime, there are lots of things you can do to improve the energy efficiency of your historic windows without compromising on design

or conservation issues. These include draught-proofing, filling any gaps with mastic or foam filler, reinstating shutters, or hanging heavy lined curtains or insulated blinds. Secondary glazing is also an option. SPAB recommends that this should be removable, unobtrusive and constructed from non-reflective glass. For thermal insulation, the ideal air gap between the existing pane and the secondary pane should be 20 mm ($^3/_4$ in). For more ideas see English Heritage's Framing Options Campaign publications.

ABOVE LEFT The windows in Grafham House, Surrey, had beautiful thin timber frames with a pointed top. Luckily most of them were saved.

RIGHT Early windows were created from multiple small pieces of glass held together with strips of lead.

A BRIEF HISTORY OF WINDOWS

Let's consider each part of the window in turn.

Window frames

Most historic window frames were made from wood. Prior to the seventeenth century, hardwood, especially oak, would have been widely used, but with the dwindling supplies of native trees, imported softwood gradually replaced hardwood. This softwood, although less durable than hardwood, was still from slow-grown, high-quality supplies from places such as Scandinavia and the Baltic States. Only in the early years of the twentieth century was high-quality softwood replaced by the quicker-growing, cheaper species of softwood that we still use today. These types of softwood are very vulnerable to decay, and need chemical treatment to make them suitable for outdoor use. Therefore, if you have a window frame made from original hardwood or old-growth softwood, it is imperative that you try to preserve it.

From the smallest pane to the largest French window, old glass should be treasured wherever it's found.

Metal window frames appeared with increasing regularity from the sixteenth century. Frames from this time are usually handmade wrought iron, and designed to hold leaded glass in either fixed or casement windows. (Fixed windows do not open, but casement windows are side-hung and designed to open inwards or outwards.) During the Victorian era cast-iron, factory-made sash windows became popular, while mild-steel windows were commonplace from around 1915 to as late as the 1970s.

Window design

Glazed windows were rare in Britain until the fifteenth century, and mainly confined to public buildings, such as churches. Owing to the difficulties of making large panes of glass, these early windows were fitted with small pieces of glass (often in diamonds or rectangles) held together with lead and set into wood or stone mullioned window frames. The earliest windows weren't designed to be opened, but this eventually changed.

Casement windows – began appearing in grander houses by the middle of the fifteenth century. Over the next three centuries this style of window slowly trickled down to more modest housing, and became a common feature in country properties. The Arts and Crafts Movement revived the fashion for casement windows in urban buildings from the 1860s onwards, when they were often decorated with beautiful stained-glass panels.

Sash windows – first appeared in the middle of the seventeenth century. Arguments rage over who invented this form of sliding window – the

The sash window – the most popular and successful window design in the history of British architecture.

Dutch, the French and the English all claim that honour – but, regardless of origins, it was a roaring success among architects and home-owners alike. The first sash windows were kept open with wooden pegs and notches, but by the early eighteenth century a clever counterweight system was developed, which allowed sash windows to stay open by themselves. Sash windows became the most popular type of window used across towns and villages for the next 200 years, although some cottages also took advantage of the 'Yorkshire slider' – a sash window laid horizontally so that it slid from side to side rather than up and down. Depending on the era and the house, sash windows can have as many as eight-over-eight or six-over-six panes of glass, or as few as two-over-two or even one-over-one. As a general rule, the more panes of glass, the older the window.

French windows – floor-length glazed windows or, more commonly, doors – were a natural extension from sash windows. They became particularly popular in the early nineteenth century because they gave home-owners easy access to fashionable features, such as their landscaped garden, conservatory or first-floor balcony.

Window glass

According to English Heritage, 'Old glass is of interest and is becoming increasingly rare. It is of value not just for its age, but because it has more richness and sparkle than today's flat sheets with their uniform reflections. Where it survives, it must be retained...' So what does historic glass look like and what kinds will you find on a restoration project?

ABOVE LEFT An early 1900s coloured pane from a stairwell window in Crouch End, London.

RIGHT Thirteenth-century glass at Old Soar Manor in Kent.

Before the early part of the nineteenth century there was only a limited choice of glass.

Crown glass – the source of most window glass, was produced by blowing and then spinning molten glass into a large, flat disc. The disc was then cut into small squares, and the quality of the glass was determined by its distance from the centre of the disc. Glass near the edge of the disc was the highest quality because it was the flattest. The glass nearer the centre was wavier and worth less. Cheapest of all was the glass at the very centre of the disc – the 'bull's eye' – where the glass blower's metal rod had been. You sometimes see dubious replicas of bull's-eye windows in country cottages and bay windows because some people think they're picturesque and authentic. The reality is that they were considered cheap and unsightly in the past; in fact, the glass blower would often throw the bull's eye back into the batch to be melted and reblown. Only stables, outbuildings and occasionally the rear windows of a humble cottage would ever use bull's-eye glass. Genuine pieces of such glass are rare these days and should be preserved. Never use fake bull's-eye glass in a restoration project.

Muff glass – was also common before the early nineteenth century. It was made by hand-blowing molten glass into an elongated balloon shape. The ends of the balloon were cut off to leave a cylinder that was then cooled, split lengthways, reheated and flattened into a rectangular shape. Muff glass is also known as 'cylinder glass'.

Both crown and muff glass are beautiful to look at and should be preserved at all costs. Their irregularity is their greatest asset because small panes of them sparkle and reflect light in a way that doesn't happen with modern glass. The bubbles, waves and other manufacturing 'defects' also give both types of glass their timeless charm. As you peer through them, the small imperfections in the glass gently distort your view (as happens in a fairground's hall of mirrors), making trees, houses and people look wonderfully wobbly.

Different versions of these two types of historic glass can be seen in historic buildings: 'rough glass', for example, is crown glass that has been rendered opaque by having its shiny surface ground down with sand and water or emery. According to Peter Nicholson's *The New Practical Builder and Workman's Companion* (1823), this type of opaque glass 'was formerly used in counting houses, &c. to prevent the inconvenience of being overlooked'.

In fact, the publication of Nicholson's book came at a turning point in the development of glass. A new variety was coming into its own, and he was very enthusiastic about it: 'Plate Glass is the most beautiful glass made use of, being nearly colourless, and sufficiently thick to admit being polished in the highest degree. The tables of this glass will admit of pieces being taken out of them much larger than can be obtained from any other...'

Plate glass – which was made by casting molten glass on to sheets of iron, removing them and then polishing the surface, was available in larger sizes than had previously been possible with crown or muff glass. This, along with the abolition of the tax by weight on glass in 1845, helped to see

In Heolas Fawr, out came the aluminium frames and in went locally made, double-glazed sash windows. In Wales you need all the insulation you can get.

an end to the manufacture of crown glass, and a boom in the production of plate glass by the end of that century. It also explains why window panes get progressively larger and glazing bars get thinner throughout this period.

Although plate glass doesn't have the inherent 'sparkle factor' of crown or muff glass, you can find some very nice examples. Nineteenth-century plate glass with bevelled edges is especially desirable.

Pressed glass – is also occasionally found in historic houses dating from the nineteenth century. This was made in a mould and often decorated in bas-relief (slightly raised) designs of vine leaves, Gothic tracery and geometric patterns. It was most often used in screens or small windows.

REPAINTING OLD WINDOWS

Hardwood window frames, especially casement windows, were often left unpainted, but softwood sash windows were almost always protected with a coat of paint. White was the most common choice for historic window frames from the eighteenth century onwards, but it wasn't the same as the bleached, brilliant whites you can buy today. Georgian whites, for example, were often actually stone- or putty-coloured.

Not all windows should be white, however. In the nineteenth century sash windows were sometimes painted dark grey, brown or green to provide a pleasing contrast with white stucco plastering. The fashion for dark frames had largely passed by the end of that century, however, when creamy white yet again became the colour of choice.

Beautiful new hardwood sash windows at Higher Hill Farm in Lancashire.

With this in mind, it can be difficult to decide what the authentic colour of a window frame should be. Manufacturers of traditional paints, such as Farrow & Ball, have a wide choice of historic colours and finishes to choose from, so it's worth spending that bit extra to get the right look. If in doubt, a historic off-white is your best bet.

As mentioned in the 'Timber' chapter, pre-1950s paint may contain lead, which is harmful when ingested or inhaled, so take extreme care if you want to remove old layers of paint from your window frames, especially if pregnant women or children live in the house. You can avoid making dangerous dust or fumes by applying a solvent-free, water-based paint remover, such as EcoStrip. Consult the Department for Environment's website (see page 246) for more information about lead in paint.

REPAIRING OLD WINDOWS

The repairs you will have to carry out on your windows depend on what materials they are made from.

Timber windows

Despite the fact that window designs have changed over the last 500 years, most repairs can still be made by a skilled joiner because the materials and construction methods have not changed that dramatically. The key is to find someone who will use traditional techniques and respect the need to conserve as much of the original frame as possible. For instance, the bottom part of a sash window is vulnerable to rot, but this doesn't necessarily mean replacing the entire frame. A new section of wood can be pieced or 'scarfed' into the area where the rotten wood has been removed. There are many companies and individuals who specialize in sash window repairs: simply look them up in Yellow Pages.

HOW TO REPLACE A SASH CORD

In their book *Period Details*, restoration experts Judith and Martin Miller explain how to replace a sash cord in nine easy steps.

1. Remove the guard beads.
2. With the lower sash raised, cut through the unbroken cords at the pulleys.
3. Remove the lower window.
4. Take off the parting beads.
5. Push up the upper window and cut through the unbroken cords.
6. Remove the upper window.
7. Take out the cover of the weight boxes in the boxed frame (at bottom of sides).
8. Note how the old cords are tied to the weights. Replace them with new cords cut to the same length: thread the cords through the pulleys and allow to drop down the hollow inside of the frame. Tie to the weights at the bottom. Nail the other ends of the cords to the grooves in the sides of the sash.
9. Replace the weight box covers and reassemble the windows by following instructions 1–6 in reverse order.

It's also important to follow the correct historical tradition for your window. When repairing timber windows, for example, remember to use the correct moulding or bevelling. Local traditions varied from county to county, so check with other historical buildings in your area, or do your own research into the vernacular traditions.

If the repair job is as simple as replacing a broken cord in a sash frame, you might want to tackle that yourself, although upstairs windows should always be repaired by professionals.

ABOVE LEFT In Grafham House, Surrey, vandals had damaged every pane of the leaded lights in the porch.

ABOVE RIGHT A sixteenth-century window from Stanway House, Gloucestershire.

Metal windows

The enemy of metal windows is corrosion. Rust should be removed carefully so as not to jeopardize the glass or underlying metal. Clean light rust either manually or with a hand-held power tool. Severe corrosion will have to be dealt with in a workshop. If repainting, choose a historically appropriate finish and colour. SPAB (see page 249) recommends alkyd resin or micaceous iron oxide paints on top of a red lead and zinc oxide primer. Any metal window repairs that require welding or similiar industrial processes should be carried out by a specialist company. For good sources see www.buildingconservation.com

REPLACING OLD GLASS

Modern float glass (so called because it is floated on to a surface of molten metal to harden) will look out of place in an historic window as it wasn't used before 1959. The lack of imperfections and mirror-like quality of float

glass make period windows look bland and will jar if placed side by side with any existing historic panes. This leaves you with two choices – either to have specialist glass made, or to attempt finding original old glass in a salvage yard. Until a few years ago it was very difficult to get crown glass because manufacturers had simply stopped producing it. Due to increasing demand, however, some UK companies have started producing versions of it again. London Crown Glass (see page 251) is a good place to start. You can also buy muff glass made in the traditional way. (Use low-ream muff glass for sixteenth-century windows and leaded lights, and no-ream muff glass for late seventeenth- to early twentieth-century windows.) The London Crown Glass company can also supply glass suitable for Georgian and Victorian properties, so you don't have to resort to modern float glass. This can be really handy for certain doors and low-level windows that need to comply with modern safety regulations.

Salvage yards are also good sources of old glass, especially if you need just to make a repair. Take along the broken pane so you can match the glass in thickness and type, and always buy more than you need to allow for any breakages. Salvage yards will also have entire windows, shutters and window furniture if you need to start from scratch or are replacing windows that were ripped out. It's worth noting, however, that windows don't like being altered. Buy the right-sized window frame or, if you are building an extension that matches the rest of your period property, build the aperture to fit the window. Proportions are key when it comes to choosing the right window, so do your research and make sure the 'new' window blends harmoniously with the rest of the house.

FAR LEFT The exterior of Strawberry Hill in London.

LEFT A heraldic shield harks back to a romanticized past.

RIGHT The house contains sumptuous interior decoration.

THE GOTHIC REVIVAL (1740–1860)

Gothic was the first truly 'home-grown' northern European architectural style. Originating in France in the mid-twelfth century, it spread right across Europe, but it was in the ecclesiastical buildings of France and England that Gothic found its most glorious expression. Some striking examples still survive today, such as Notre Dame and Sainte Chapelle in Paris, and King's College Chapel in Cambridge.

For many people, the word 'Gothic' conjures up images of tall pointed churches and cathedrals. This over-simplification actually cuts to the very heart of Gothic: these buildings allowed mankind to reach for the heavens in praise of the Lord. Structure was stripped to a minimum, and buildings became architectural exercises in getting the least amount of stone to soar to the greatest height. Huge openings were punctured in church walls and filled with beautiful stained glass. Streaming with sunlight, these colourful windows were the Hollywood movies of their day, awing the masses with biblical and religious tales. As well as their vast interior spaces and stained glass, Gothic buildings were also characterized by lancets (pointed arches), foils (leaf-shaped designs) and decorative carvings in the form of gargoyles, heads, animals and leaves.

For centuries, Gothic reigned as the 'style supreme' for ecclesiastical and public buildings. But change was afoot. By the late fourteenth and early fifteenth centuries the Renaissance was emerging in Italy: new scientific ideas, new art, new sculpture and a new architectural style would change the world. Living among the remnants of the Roman civilization had led the godfathers of the Renaissance first to idealize this vanished empire, then to adopt its architectural style. Gothic designs were marginalized in favour of the columns, rounded arches and mathematical symmetry of Roman buildings. The spread of these new ideas was unprecedented. By the early sixteenth century, classical architecture had replaced Gothic as the dominant style in Britain, and was being fully embraced by leading architects, such as Inigo Jones and Christopher Wren.

LEFT No surface or fitting is left undecorated in Strawberry Hill.

RIGHT The early 'Gothick' additions at Strawberry Hill began as pastiche, but over time details were increasingly copied from original Gothic examples.

Classicism remained popular well into the Georgian period, but the great cathedrals, churches and civic buildings were constant reminders of our Gothic past. Britain was also beginning to rule the waves. Its trade and territories in the New World were creating huge wealth, and with it came a new confidence, self-belief and nationalistic zeal. Some in Britain felt the country should no longer look to the Continent for design ideas and historical inspiration.

Mid-eighteenth-century writers and artists began to create a sentimental view of the medieval era, glorifying the period as one of romance, pageantry and breathtaking architecture. The Gothic buildings of the Middle Ages represented Britain's long and proud history of freedom and Christianity. It was time for the Gothic style to be 'revived'.

Early attempts at re-created medieval Gothic architecture and interiors were essentially pastiches and light-hearted in character – a trait that earned them the title 'Gothick'. They bore little resemblance to the true traditions of medieval Gothic styling, and presented an over-romanticized, sentimental view of the past. Nowhere was this more true than in the Gothick follies and faux ruins that appeared in landscaped gardens, such as Shotover in Oxfordshire and Stowe in Buckinghamshire. Beyond the attractive vistas that these 'pretend ruins' provided, the asymmetry of this new style appealed to garden designers, who were starting to revel in breaking the rigid formal rules of classicism.

Typical patrons of this new style of architecture were wealthy aristocrats for whom the choice of a Gothick home was a clear statement about their artistic and cultural sensibilities. One of the great houses from this period is Strawberry Hill in Twickenham, Middlesex. Built between 1750 and 1790 by Horace Walpole, son of the prime minister Robert Walpole, it is the embodiment of lavish Gothick taste. Not only does it feature heraldic stained glass, medieval-style fireplaces and gilded ceilings, but the exterior experiments with all the

ideas and designs that would come to dominate the later, historically accurate, Gothic Revival: battlements, quatrefoil and lancet windows, buttresses and asymmetry.

By the beginning of the nineteenth century, however, frivolous Gothick had given way to a more serious attempt to re-create Gothic architecture. The new-found popularity of archaeology, combined with a rigorous academic study of the past, resulted in a more historically accurate 'Gothic Revival' style. The choice of Augustus Pugin and Charles Barry's Gothic design to replace the Houses of Parliament in 1836 gave Gothic Revival the impetus to become the symbol of the Victorian age. Other great public buildings soon followed, and 'the magnificent science of its structure', as John Ruskin wrote, appealed to the Victorians, who seized on the structurally expressive nature of Gothic to articulate their new-found engineering prowess. The great railway stations, town halls and museums of the day would combine brick, stone and iron in a way that is still spellbinding 150 years later.

But Gothic Revival, unlike the original medieval Gothic style, had a profound effect on domestic buildings too. Many ordinary houses from the early nineteenth century have unmistakably Gothic details, designed to bring a touch of the baronial style to towns and cities. Look out for: pointed doorways and windows; Victorian fake beams; stone or wood fireplaces carved into an arch; brass or iron wall sconces and chandeliers; wall tapestries; encaustic floor tiles (Minton tiles were often given heraldic motifs); original heavily patterned wallpaper with coats of arms, fleurs-de-lis or other medieval designs; oak panelling and furniture. These hallmarks of Gothic Revival, sometimes known as Victorian Gothic, survive in many buildings around the UK.

BRICKS

Many of us associate bricks with smoky Victorian terraces of the Industrial Revolution, but they have a longer and more illustrious history than you might imagine. Fired bricks have actually been around for thousands of years: the Sumerians were building brick houses, temples and towers 3000 years before the birth of Christ, and the first bricks to hit British shores came with the Roman occupation in the first century AD.

The Romans were dab hands at making, firing and building with bricks; in fact, you can still see examples of their handiwork at places such as Burgh Castle in Norfolk. However, all their know-how was lost when the crumbling Roman Empire abandoned Britain in the middle of the fifth century. Although remnants of Romano-British buildings remained, these were often plundered by local tribes looking for free building materials. In fact, many of the buildings of this little-understood period in history contain reused Roman bricks, St Albans Cathedral and Holy Trinity Church in Colchester being two of the most famous examples.

In other parts of the world, however, brick-making technology was alive and well. In places such as Persia, Italy and the Netherlands brick continued to be used with great flair, and, thanks to increased foreign trade and travel, the art of brick-making finally returned to Britain in the thirteenth century. The fashion for brick buildings grew in the south and east of the country – some of the earliest post-Roman brick buildings are in East Anglia – but bricks remained a costly and rare luxury well into the fifteenth century. Brick palaces from this time, such as Tattershall Castle in Lincolnshire and Faulkbourne Hall in Essex, were considered the epitome of expensive taste and cutting-edge design. Less wealthy families might

From Roman walls, *above right*, to Arts and Crafts houses, *left*, bricks have played a vital role in Britain's building history.

ABOVE Herringbone brick infills in a sixteenth-century timber-framed house.

LEFT Early handmade bricks at Tattershall Castle in Lincolnshire.

replace the wattle and daub panels on their timber-framed houses with trendy brick infills, but for most of the population this useful building material would remain out of financial reach for another 200 years.

During the seventeenth and eighteenth centuries, Britain experienced a rapid growth in its towns and cities. The Industrial Revolution was in its infant stages, encouraging people to leave their rural surroundings and flock to urban centres in search of work. Burgeoning populations were finding themselves crammed into crowded, timber-framed buildings. Fire was a constant threat in such conditions, and it's no coincidence that brick enjoyed a huge surge in popularity after the Great Fire of London in 1666. From that point on, all efforts were made to ensure that as many London buildings as possible were constructed from stone or brick and used a minimum of flammable timber. The regions were soon to follow. The golden age of brick building had arrived.

WHAT MAKES OLD BRICKS SO BEAUTIFUL?

In the past, brick-making was a complex, time-consuming process, and this explains why old bricks are so wonderfully varied in colour, shape and texture.

The raw ingredients of a brick are sand, clay and water. Before the 1850s these three ingredients were mixed either by hand or by animals driving a heavy roller around a mixing pit. The result was often unevenly mixed and, when fired, produced subtle variations in colour and texture. After the introduction of mechanized mixing machines in the middle of the nineteenth century, bricks became much more evenly coloured and textured.

Brick variations also arose from the type of clay used. Before the advent of a cohesive transport system in the Victorian era, bricks were made mostly from local clays. These varied in their chemical and mineral composition, resulting in different coloured bricks. Ferric oxide gives bricks their traditional red and orange colours, for example, while the presence of lime creates a creamy yellow. Bricks were also coloured artificially. For example, if a clay did not contain enough limestone to produce a creamy colour, builders often added chalk to the basic sand and clay mix to produce a whitish-yellow brick. In the mid-eighteenth century pale brick colours were all the rage.

Look closely at the type of bond, the mortar and the colour of your bricks. Are they handmade or machine-produced?

Colour variation in old bricks also depended on the firing process and where the bricks were placed in the kiln. Restricting the oxygen in the kiln, for example, produces a blue tinge, resulting in bricks often known as Staffordshire blues. Even when using consistent clays in modern kilns, tiny differences in temperature and oxygen supply create different-coloured bricks, including yellows, pinks, and purples. During the eighteenth century, when the technology changed from rudimentary wood-fired kilns to more fuel-efficient, coal-fired kilns, one type of brick became very popular. 'Vitrified' bricks, which were placed so close to the source of heat that they became glazed, were a common by-product of the new firing process, and people enjoyed their decorative potential. These glassy bricks look terrific, especially in conjunction with red bricks, when laid in chequered, chevron or lozenge patterns. Sometimes vitrified bricks were used to create complete façades to houses.

LEFT Huge brick chimneystacks were a favourite in Tudor times.

RIGHT A fine example of Elizabethan brickwork at Otley Hall in Suffolk.

Old bricks are also uneven in terms of shape and thickness. Prior to the 1830s, all bricks were made by hand. The clay mix was thrown into a wooden mould (called a 'strike'), then tipped out and left to dry before being fired. This hand-making process inevitably produced slight variations in texture and thickness, but a more significant factor is that brick sizes were not truly standardized until the beginning of the twentieth century. The area of a brick varies very little from region to region and throughout time, but there are huge differences in the thickness of old bricks. Pre-seventeenth-century bricks are often 50 mm (2 in) thick or less; eighteenth-century bricks are a little thicker; and nineteenth-century bricks are around 65 mm ($2^1/_2$ in). However, these measures are not hard and fast. Early medieval 'great bricks', for example, are only 45 mm ($1^3/_4$ in) thick, but covered a much bigger area than other bricks. Extra large bricks were also used on building projects between 1784 and 1803, when a brick tax was imposed according to the number of bricks used in a building.

The industrious Victorians much improved brick technology, and during this period more bricks were produced than in any other era. Developments in manufacturing allowed bricks to be made with greater accuracy, speed and colour variation, while advances in transport meant that they could be conveyed anywhere in the country, leading to a decline in local brick traditions. However, even as late as World War II, most bricks were still made within a 50-km (30-mile) radius of their destination.

Mortar mixes also changed during this time. Quicker, stronger formulations, such as Portland cement, which became popular after 1850, allowed huge civil engineering and housing projects to take place at speed.

Brickwork detail from Quarry Bank cotton mill in Cheshire.

Flemish garden wall bond

Also known as Sussex bond, this is a version of Flemish bond that served the same function as English garden wall bond. It is made by using one header brick every three stretcher bricks.

Variations on these five types of bonds are common in old buildings. Look closely at the rest of your house to see what patterns have been used, and keep any new work sympathetic. If you are starting from scratch, a quick look at adjacent houses in your street, or a bit of research in the local history section of your library, will tell you a lot about the different bonding trends in your area.

WHAT CAN GO WRONG WITH OLD BRICKS?

Bricks are tough and can last thousands of years, but it's not unusual to find different levels of deterioration in historic brickwork. There are lots of reasons why bricks fail (see box opposite).

CLEANING HISTORIC BRICKWORK

Bricks appreciate the gentle touch. As mentioned earlier, over-abrasive forms of cleaning, such as sandblasting or high-pressure water jets, can damage the valuable surface of brick, leaving it open to further problems. The same applies to many chemical cleaners, which are just too strong for old brickwork. Any chemical applications are best undertaken by a

REASONS FOR BRICK FAILURE

- **The original bricks were too soft.** This could be because they were badly made or underfired, causing them to crumble over time.
- **The bricks have become saturated with water** (often as a result of a leaky gutter or drainpipe). During a frosty spell, the trapped water expands, causing the bricks to shatter.
- **Water saturation** can also cause the mortar to erode, affecting the structural strength of the wall.
- **Brick clay often contains soluble salts.** Even after firing, some of these salts remain in the brick. If a brick gets repeatedly wet, the salts can travel to just below the surface of the brick, causing the surface to crumble and flake off. This is called 'cryptoflorescence', and often occurs in poorly fired bricks sitting in damp areas, such as cellars.
- **Acid rain damages brick.** The pollution not only eats away at the lime mortar between the bricks, but can also lead to actual damage on the face of the brickwork.
- **Metal wall ties and other reinforcements** in brickwork can rust, expand and cause damage to the surrounding material.
- **Inappropriate mortar repairs will damage brickwork.** Old bricks expand and need the surrounding mortar to be soft enough to accommodate this movement. Modern Portland cement-based mortars are too hard for most historic bricks. Use a soft, lime-based mortar on any brickwork that pre-dates 1850 (see page 63).
- **Sandblasting old brickwork exposes it to harm.** Bricks have an outer surface called a 'fireskin', which protects the softer, more permeable inner brick from water penetration. Very abrasive cleaning methods, such as sandblasting and gritblasting, remove this precious outer skin and leave the bricks vulnerable to water damage and decay.
- **Modern paints and water-repellent coatings** are not advisable for historic brickwork. They often lack breathability and will trap moisture within a wall, causing long-term damage.
- **Bad pointing.** Certain types of modern pointing, such as ribbon pointing, which stands proud of the brick, encourage water to collect on and penetrate the surface of the brickwork. This type of pointing also looks unsightly and is historically inaccurate.
- **Rampant vegetation.** Ivy can penetrate joints and cracks in brickwork or crumbling lime mortar. If you don't want to remove your ivy, make sure it is kept in check with regular pruning and doesn't start to invade guttering and downpipes (it will block them and cause them to leak). If you do want to get rid of any ivy, be extremely careful, as yanking it can pull the mortar out too. Consult a conservation expert, who will be able to assess whether it's better to leave the ivy in place rather than attempt to remove it.
- **Structural problems.** Subsidence, structural failures, tree roots, vibration, failure of lintels or joists – all these problems can have serious consequences for brickwork. Always consult a structural engineer if you suspect your building might be unstable, and don't attempt any repairs until the underlying problem is solved.

specialist conservation contractor, who will have all the appropriate safety equipment and correct dilutions for historic brickwork.

In most cases, however, the best approach is to remove any dirt or grime gently with a soft bristle brush, a mild detergent and warm water (although, as with stonework, don't do this when there's a risk of frost). Rinse thoroughly with clean water. Be careful not to scrub too hard on delicate areas of brickwork, such as carved decorations. For soot or greasy stains, steam cleaning is a good option but is best carried out by a professional. Be aware, however, that all water-based methods of cleaning can cause temporary efflorescence (harmless white salt deposits, which can be brushed off).

For all types of brick cleaning, SPAB recommend that you first conduct an on-site trial. See the 'Stonework' chapter for more information about cleaning masonry.

Redbrick and terracotta, *above*, and decorative diapered brickwork, *right*.

REPAIRING HISTORIC BRICKWORK

In all restoration projects you should work on the principle of minimum intervention because this helps to preserve as much of the original historic building as possible. The first thing to do is to establish what's causing the problem: it could be something as simple as leaky guttering or some missing pointing.

Once you've established the cause of the problem and made the appropriate changes, you might not need to carry out any further repairs. The brickwork might be best left alone. However, if the damaged

The mechanization of brick production allowed for the large-scale construction of terraces such as these miners' houses in Easington, Durham.

brickwork is threatening the structural integrity of the building or allowing water to penetrate, it's time to make a conservation repair. Only in the direst of circumstances should brickwork be taken down and rebuilt because – as explained in the section about bonding – it can be impossible to recreate the look of very old brickwork. Organizations such as English Heritage and SPAB have some very useful publications about repairing brickwork, and may be able to help you find a suitable conservation contractor. Check out SPAB's pamphlets 'Repointing Stone and Brick Walling' and 'Removing Paint from Old Buildings', both produced in 2002.

Any repointing of old brickwork should be carried out with an appropriate mortar (see 'Lime' chapter). As a general rule, any building pre-1850 will need a lime-based mortar in a ratio of 1:3, 1:4 or 1:5 lime to sand. The odd damaged brick can be replaced by simply raking out the mortar and turning the brick around. This will only be possible with lime mortar,

however, as hard cement mortar is very difficult to remove. SPAB doesn't currently recommend the use of plastic repairs (see page 120) to hide decayed brick faces, as they could damage adjoining brickwork.

If you need to replace entire bricks, you have two choices: new handmade bricks or salvaged ones. Neither option is cheap, but modern, machine-made bricks are simply not up to the job. There are several companies around the country making good-quality handmade bricks using traditional methods and kilns. A quick trawl of the Internet should locate your nearest supplier. Take along a sample and they will be able to match the colour and texture of your old bricks, although any replacements will obviously look new compared to the old weathered bricks. Artificial weathering – which involves distressing or applying fake finishes to modern bricks to give the appearance of ageing – never looks truly authentic and is not recommended. Reclaimed bricks are also an option, although you have to be certain that they are of high enough quality to withstand weathering (some bricks designed for internal use are of poorer quality and will not withstand the elements). For external walls you will need bricks that are classed as at least moderately frost-resistant, while for areas that are constantly subjected to water (such as window sills and paving) you will need totally frost-resistant bricks. If unsure of the type you need, consult a builder who knows about old bricks.

Avoid any bricks that are damaged or covered in paint. Whether you go for new or salvaged bricks, always buy more than you need (roughly 10 per cent of the total amount) so that you have enough to cover inevitable wastage and future repairs.

ABOVE LEFT Detail from William Morris's Red House.

RIGHT A brick and tile-hung late Victorian villa in Henley-on-Thames, Oxfordshire.

Three examples that show the eclectic nature of Victorian design: Tudor revival at Mentmore Towers, *far left*, the French-style chateau at Waddesdon Manor, *left*, and the Italian style of Osborne House, *opposite*.

VICTORIAN CONSERVATION AND CHANGE (1840–1901)

Two seemingly contradictory features dominate Victorian domestic architecture: one is that most Victorian houses are incredibly similar, built in repetitive brick terraces; the other is that within this monotony lies a surprising amount of individuality and creativity.

The Victorian era was a time of great change. The British Empire was expanding at breakneck speed, while increased foreign trade brought with it exotic products, exotic materials and, most importantly of all, exotic ideas. One of the immediate results of this new 'global awareness' was a splintering of design taste. In the Georgian period, ideas of style had been fairly unified and straightforward – classicism reigned supreme. In the Victorian age, however, people became much more aware and interested in the different styles from both present and past, Britain and abroad.

Correspondingly, the great country houses built at this time are hugely eclectic in their styling. Osborne House, Queen Victoria's home on the Isle of Wight, copied the style of an Italianate villa, for example, while in Buckinghamshire Mentmore Towers and Waddesdon emulated Elizabethan and French chateau architecture respectively. Other great houses embraced Gothic, Renaissance, Greek, Romanesque and Baroque revivals as the increasingly liberated minds of architects produced an incredible range of styles for the upper end of the social spectrum.

Despite the eclectic ideas used in the design of these country estates, most of us associate Victorian housing with repetition – row upon row of identical houses. One of the main reasons for this repetitiveness was the sudden ubiquitous use of red brick. Technological developments and advances in the rail network broke an age-old reliance on local materials. Suddenly, hard, durable and uniformly shaped bricks could be cheaply mass-produced and transported around the country for the first time. The sheer numbers of dwellings built by each developer and the need to comply with stricter building regulations also added to the uniform appearance of Victorian housing. A typical nineteenth-century terraced house was the

same whether you lived in London or Liverpool – two rooms deep by one room wide. Rarely did the frontage of the house exceed 8 metres (25 ft). Bigger versions of this plan were achieved by adding on an attic, cellar or back extension, but the basic scheme remained the same. Within this apparent monotony, however, there were touches of genuine creativity and invention.

The new ideas expressed in the architecture of grand country houses began to trickle down to middle-class homes. If you take a closer look at Victorian terraces, you can pick out the same range of revivalist and exotic influences: the rounded arches and flat-pitched roofline of Italianate; the large, ornate Dutch gables of Queen Anne; or the banded brickwork, pointed dormers and windows of the Gothic Revival (see page 151). Terraces with bay windows turned away from the monumentality of the Georgian age to emphasize the individuality of each house, not to mention the status of the proud new owner.

Within the interior of the Victorian house, there existed the same conflict between conservatism and new ideas. Social interaction and behaviour were highly formalized in the Victorian era; public and private life were carefully compartmentalized, resulting in a complex daily routine that was deeply engrained in households of all sizes. Even relaxing at home was regimented, with different parts of the day spent in specific parts of the house and certain meals eaten only in certain rooms. The result for the middle-class home was a layout dominated by corridors and

RIGHT Dark, cluttered and highly decorated, Victorian interiors were the antithesis of today's minimalist style.

BELOW LEFT The ubiquitous red-brick terrace. But study terraces closely and you will find a wealth of variation, such as the Queen Anne touches to this London terrace.

small rooms. Everything was planned to create barriers between parts of daily life – even down to the way that doors opened. Doors in Victorian properties always swung into the room to obscure the view as one entered. This gave the occupants of the room time to ready themselves for the new arrival.

The feeling of claustrophobia inherent in the design of these houses was heightened by the prevailing taste of the day. Victorians, as we know, liked a mishmash of styles, so could never be described as minimalists. Architects and households also had a wealth of new materials and consumer goods that mass production and fashion put within their reach. The results could be overcomplicated and over-ornate, but also hugely experimental and radical. Heavy, dark colours were combined with highly decorative patterns, wallpapers and curtains. Every surface or object was loaded with decoration, and every available tabletop or ledge crammed with ornaments and knick-knacks. Rooms were literally stuffed to the brim with decoration.

Victorian domestic architecture was very much the result of mass production, but if you look past this superficial uniformity, you can find richness and variety, a playfulness, worldliness and quality that shames the majority of new houses built today. While the humble brick is thought of as the lowest common denominator in terms of building materials, it's hard to look at the diagonal brick arches of Victorian viaducts and tunnels, the rubbed brick details on some late Victorian buildings or the vast brick walls of the great rail terminals and not be moved by their beauty.

ARCHITECTURAL METALWORK

The purpose of this chapter is to give a quick run-through of the most common types of architectural metalwork you're likely to find in an old house. You'll discover how to tell your brass from your bronze, what causes metals to decay, and how to go about putting things right. For each type of metal you'll see that the approaches can vary quite dramatically, so it's really important to have a general grasp of the basics. Although there is much that you can do yourself, the conservation of valuable or historically significant metalwork should always be undertaken by a professional.

RUST GLORIOUS RUST

First, a little bit about metals in general. Few metals come directly from nature in a usable form. Instead, they are dug up as mineral ores from which the metal is extracted, often using very high temperatures. The resulting metal product is more usable, but also more unstable, and will slowly begin to deteriorate as it attempts to revert back to its original mineral ore state. This is why metals corrode.

Not all corrosion is bad, however. A layer of corrosion that is even and stable can actually protect the metal underneath from further harm, and provide a pleasing aesthetic effect. This is known as 'uniform corrosion' or patina (from the Latin word *patens*, the name of the Roman copper dishes that developed a characteristic green layer of corrosion). In other cases, however, corrosion is unstable and destructive, eating away at the fabric of the metal object with devastating consequences. The trick is to know the difference between patina and unwanted corrosion.

From the smallest handle to the largest gate, if your house predates 1700 you'll probably find some interesting examples of wrought iron.

Ironwork – the most common form of architectural metalwork in any historic house.

ALLOY, ALLOY

To make metals more useful we combine them with others. A combination of more than one metal is called an 'alloy'; bronze, for example, is an alloy of copper, tin and zinc. Alloys that consist of just two metals are called 'binary alloys', those containing three metals are 'tertiary alloys', and so on. Mixing metals in this way often improves their hardness, strength, flexibility or casting properties, but it can also bring its own particular problems, as explained later.

IRONWORK

In most period homes ironwork will be the main type of architectural metalwork, and will pop up in everything from gates to gazebos and railings to radiators.

In its purest form, iron is a soft, grey metal that is tough yet flexible. A simple way of making things from it was simply to heat it up and bash it into various shapes. This is known as 'wrought iron' (the word wrought means 'worked') and has been used in Britain since about 1000 BC. The art of the blacksmith is centred on wrought iron, and throughout most of history he would have been a vital part of village life, producing everything from hoes to horseshoes. If your house predates 1700, the chances are that any ironwork in it will be wrought iron.

Making cast iron involved a more sophisticated technique, namely, heating it until liquid and pouring it into a mould to set. In Britain,

archaeological evidence suggests that people have been attempting to make furnaces hot enough to produce molten iron since Saxon times, while researchers found evidence that the Cistercian monks of Rievaulx Abbey, Yorkshire, were developing a prototype blast furnace for the large-scale production of cast iron when they were evicted by King Henry VIII in 1538. It wasn't until the early eighteenth century, however, that the technology became available to make cast iron a widespread commercial reality.

Wrought-iron balconies and porches at Oxford Parade in Cheltenham.

There are pros and cons to both types of iron. Wrought iron is labour-intensive to make, but malleable and strong, with a fibrous structure – perfect for the fine details on decorative metalwork. Cast iron is easier and quicker to make as it is a more industrialized, repetitive process, but it is more brittle and weaker under tension than wrought iron.

So what things were made from wrought and cast iron? During the seventeenth and eighteenth centuries gates, balconies and staircases were all fashioned from wrought iron. Its easy workability meant that highly creative and individual designs could be produced. Robert Bakewell, one of England's best-known ironsmiths from that era, made a magnificent wrought-iron arbour (known as 'the birdcage'), which is still standing at Melbourne Hall in Derbyshire. You can also see a series of his fabulous wrought-iron gates outside Derby Cathedral and Derby Industrial Museum.

Cast iron, which was poured into predetermined moulds, was perfect for mass-produced designs, such as railings, guttering, columns, fireplaces, baths, window frames, garden benches and conservatories. From the end of the eighteenth century, when casting techniques became more sophisticated, cast iron largely replaced wrought iron in most

LEFT Elaborate iron gates at John Part Almshouses in Derbyshire.

RIGHT The door knocker at Brasenose Gate, Stamford in Lincolnshire.

building applications. Most ironwork on houses later than 1800 will be cast iron, although railings and gates on smarter houses may still have been individually commissioned in wrought iron. Original wrought ironwork is now very desirable and can fetch high prices in auctions and salvage yards.

Cleaning and restoring ironwork

The main problem with iron is that it corrodes when exposed to water and oxygen (wrought iron corrodes more easily than cast iron). So if you want to keep your historic ironwork in tip-top condition, you have to clean it the right way and protect it from the elements.

If you need to shift grime from ironwork, never use water, as this will encourage corrosion. Use methylated spirits or paraffin instead, and rub away the dirt with a cloth. If the item you are cleaning is small and has really stubborn grime, you can leave it to soak in meths or paraffin for 24 hours, then gently scrub away the dirt with very fine wire wool.

If rust has started to appear, you can easily tackle it with a commercial rust remover and fine steel wool (just follow the manufacturer's instructions). Another good option is a product called Renaissance Metal De-corroder (see page 251), a conservation-approved, non-toxic system for rust removal. The treatment selectively ruptures the bond between the iron and the corrosion layer, reducing rust to a sludge that is easily wiped or brushed away.

You'll need to seal any de-rusted ironwork to prevent further problems. Choose a suitable exterior or interior sealant depending on the location of the architectural feature. If you want to use the traditional method, boiled

Beautiful metalwork isn't just confined to the house, as this exquisite iron garden seat at William Morris's Red House demonstrates.

linseed oil can be very effective. Simply apply, leave for ten minutes, then buff off the excess.

To repaint exterior ironwork, first make sure it is free from rust, oil or grease. Use a rust protector, two coats of primer and one or two final coats all from the same manufacturer – this prevents any problems with compatibility between paint types. Primers recommended in the past by conservation experts include red lead, zinc phosphate, zinc chromate or zinc dust primer, but take advice from an ironwork restoration expert on this as new developments in paints are always appearing on the market (see the Building Conservation Directory, page 246).

Interior ironwork, such as fireplaces, grates or balusters, will buff up nicely with a commercial polish, such as Zebo Black Grate Polish or something similar, and a soft cloth.

You can remove old layers of paint from both wrought and cast iron with a paint stripper. Chemical strippers are fine, but you can also get eco-friendly paint strippers that will do just the same job with fewer harmful side effects. EcoStrip is the best known of these eco options. More abrasive methods, such as shotblasting or sandblasting, are fine for cast iron (provided it's not too thin), but should never be used on wrought iron because they remove the precious 'mill scale' layer, which provides a natural barrier against corrosion. If paint residues are being removed, take great care to protect yourself from breathing in highly toxic dust from old lead paints (see 'Timber' chapter).

More serious corrosion, where the fabric of the ironwork has been eaten away, will have to be repaired professionally using welding or metal stitching. Consult a cast-iron foundry or restoration expert about this.

Lead is resistant to frost and corrosion, making it the perfect material for outdoor items such as rainwater goods and planters.

Wrought iron will need to be mended using different techniques from those for cast iron. Blacksmiths are few and far between, but are worth hunting down because they are a wonderful source of advice and practical expertise. Repairs to wrought iron should be like with like – in other words, don't mix materials such as steel or cast iron with wrought iron. These three materials have different rates of corrosion, and both cast iron and steel lack the handmade charm of wrought iron.

LEAD

Another common metal found in old houses is lead. Being very soft and malleable, it is easy to bend into shapes, and surprisingly resistant to corrosion and frost. For this reason it has been used on the exteriors of old buildings, especially for roofs and guttering. It was also commonly used for pipework inside the home.

The problem with lead, as we all know, is that it's very poisonous. As a result, many lead pipes have been removed from old houses and replaced with modern, non-toxic substitutes. This course of action is probably the best strategy, although some conservation experts believe that unless your water supply is highly acidic, there is very little risk of lead leaching into it and causing poisoning. British Water advises that property owners who want to check lead levels in their mains supply should contact their water supplier or local environmental health officer. If significant lead levels are found in the supply, the normal solution is to remove the lead pipework completely. In the short-term, however, a drinking water filter fitted to the water supply, or a reverse osmosis system, will substantially reduce lead levels.

Restoring lead

Working with lead is another area where common sense has to prevail. You can safely remove paint from the surface of lead using a chemical stripper in poultice form, but you must be careful to avoid creating dust or fumes, as these are the two commonest ways that lead can enter the body. (Lead is not usually absorbed through the skin, except in the form of lead alkyls, which are added to petrol, so if you handle cold metallic lead you will not get lead poisoning.) Any work with lead objects that is likely to create dust or fumes, such as sanding or drilling, needs to be carried out (or at least assessed) by a lead restoration expert, who will have the latest recommendations on the best practice for health and safety (see the Building Conservation Directory, page 246). Also read the leaflet 'Lead and You – A Guide to Working Safely with Lead' (INDG305) available from the Health and Safety Executive (see page 247).

Lead roofs in particular can suffer from a number of faults. One of the most common is when soft lead sheets distort under their own weight and begin to droop. This is called 'creep', and can also be seen on large lead garden ornaments, such as urns and troughs. Lead also likes to expand and contract with heat. If lead roof tiles are fixed incorrectly, leaving no room to accommodate expansion movement, they will tend to crack and let in water. If lead roof tiles are too thin, or laid on a horizontal surface, they also have a tendency to allow water to penetrate the building.

Brass's lovely creamy gold colour has made it a popular material for expensive details such as locks, *above left*, and fingerplates, *above right*.

With all these problems it's best to take professional advice. Lead roofs that pre-date 1850 will be made from cast lead rather than the more modern milled lead, which is thought to be tougher and more long lasting. If you need to make replacements, consider using cast lead instead of milled lead, and don't be tempted to skimp on costs: thin lead tiles can let in water and prove a false economy. DIY repairs using materials such as solder will not solve the problem long-term, and in many cases actually make the situation worse. Sealing your lead roof with a layer of waterproof bitumen, for example, will trap moisture, causing timber decay and condensation. In addition, as bitumen is virtually impossible to remove once applied, it will eventually mean that the entire lead roof has to be replaced.

BRASS

Brass is an alloy made from copper and zinc, and is fairly resistant to corrosion. This has made it a favourite for expensive-looking taps, showers, door furniture and window latches.

Cleaning and restoring brass

Some people like to keep their brassware shiny and looking new; others like to leave it to develop a mellow patina. The patina actually protects the brass underneath, so it's always worth considering whether an item needs polishing. Brass can also darken if you apply too much polish. In addition, certain objects are just brass-plated, and over-rigorous cleaning will remove the finish completely, exposing the base metal underneath.

If you want to clean brass, always do a patch test first on an area as inconspicuous as possible. Commercial cleaners, such as Brasso and Vulpex Liquid Soap, are perfect for the job. To prevent further tarnishing or corrosion you can finish the surface with Renaissance Wax, a restoration product first developed by the British Museum, which is now used in museums and stately homes around the world. (For product suppliers, see page 251.) Very old or expensive brass items, especially if they are in bad condition, will require special care. A museum expert or metal restorer will be able to help you with this.

Old brass was sometimes coated in clear lacquer to prevent it from tarnishing. If this layer has failed and begun to peel away, you can remove it with acetone (nail polish remover). You may then reapply a clear lacquer, but conservationists prefer to use a wax finish, such as Renaissance (see above).

BRONZE

An alloy usually consisting of copper, tin and zinc, bronze tends to be more expensive than brass, and is used less often around the home. However, you do find bronze window and door furniture, as well as bronze statues and ornaments.

Cleaning and restoring bronze

Like brass, bronze is relatively resistant to corrosion. Over time it develops an attractive green patina, but it will deteriorate rapidly if exposed to excess

Brass bath taps, *above left*, and a bronze door hook, *above right*.

moisture or chemical pollutants. The best way to care for old bronze is to keep it clean and dry, and dust regularly with a soft, lint-free cloth. (Dust that settles on any type of metal will attract moisture and encourage corrosion.)

If a bronze item needs more than dusting, you can remove layers of grime with a soft brush. Alternatively, you could try using a restoration-approved product, such as Vulpex Liquid Soap, or a weak solution of salty water. Rinse and dry thoroughly.

A clear lacquer is often applied to bronze to prevent tarnishing. If this layer is sound, all the item will need is the occasional rub with a soft cloth. If the layer has worn away or is peeling off, look into getting it replaced. The Building Conservation Directory (see page 246) has a list of reputable products and companies that will carry out such work on your behalf.

As for polishing bronze, that depends on whether you like the patina or not. Patinas are highly prized, so you may be knocking value off objects by removing them. One complicating factor is that many items apparently made of solid bronze are in fact just bronze-plated and should never be polished. Take advice if you are at all uncertain.

'Bronze disease' is a common and serious problem with antique bronze. If you see pale green, powdery crystals forming on the surface, this is a sign that the bronze is being attacked by excessive moisture or has come into contact with ground salts. Professional advice should be taken, as the item will need to be treated with chemicals in a controlled environment, such as a laboratory.

COPPER

You probably won't find much copper around a period home, but just in case, here's a little bit about this lovely metal.

In its natural state, copper has a pinky-orange hue, but soon tarnishes to brown on exposure to the atmosphere. Left to corrode, it will develop a blue-green colour. Its softness allows it to be rolled or hammered into sheets, which are then easily turned into attractive objects, including pots and pans for the kitchen. Copper is also a great conductor of electricity and heat, hence its continuing use in wiring and plumbing systems. If you are really lucky, you may have a copper bath. Before cast iron became especially popular in the mid-nineteenth century, rolltop baths in smart houses were sometimes made from copper. These are highly collectable in today's market, and should be conserved at all costs. Copper also enjoyed a brief revival during the Arts and Crafts period (1860–1925) and the Art

LEFT Copper is soft enough to be hammered into sheets and line kitchen sinks.

ABOVE RIGHT With its heat-conducting properties, copper makes the ideal material for kitchenware.

Nouveau period (1890–1914), when it was employed to make magnificently decorative hammered or moulded copper fire surrounds. Again, these are valuable architectural antiques and should be preserved if possible.

Cleaning and restoring copper

The brownish patina that copper develops over time is considered to be desirable by most people, but as soon as green crystals start to form and corrode the metal, it's time to take action. Copper is also susceptible to another form of corrosion (caused by organic acids), which results in a dark green waxy layer called verdigris. Although not entirely welcome, verdigris won't harm your copper object, and can be easily shifted with methylated spirits on a soft rag.

Warning: Verdigris is poisonous, so you should always wear disposable gloves when cleaning copper. Copper dust is also harmful, so avoid doing anything that creates copper powder.

If you want to clean copper, a traditional copper polish will bring it up nicely, and you can choose either to wax it or seal it with lacquer. See page 251 for recommended products.

For further information on conserving all types of historic metals, consult English Heritage's *Practical Building Conservation: Metals Vol. 4* by John and Nicola Ashurst. Although currently out of print, this book is still available through Amazon, or can be bought second-hand from architectural bookshops.

From stained glass and wallpaper, *left*, to Red House, *opposite*, the Arts and Crafts Movement is dominated by William Morris. Very few designers have had such a huge impact on British culture.

ARTS, CRAFTS AND CONTRADICTIONS (1860–1910)

The Arts and Crafts Movement is perhaps best known for the textiles and wallpapers of William Morris. In fact, his beautiful floral patterns still adorn sofas and walls in millions of homes. As a driving force behind the movement, Morris not only changed the face of interior decoration, but also inspired a whole new approach to architecture.

The Arts and Crafts Movement grew from the writings of Augustus Pugin and John Ruskin, the two leading figures of the Gothic Revival (see page 151). But whereas the Gothic Revival focused on great churches and cathedrals, Morris was fascinated by the simple beauty of medieval cottages, almshouses and barns. His imagination was captured by the principles of functionality, honest construction and the use of local materials, combined with the ideal of craftsmen freely expressing themselves through the act of building. Morris rejected mass production and the use of machinery, which he felt reduced factory workers to nothing more than slaves. Indeed, it's no coincidence that the Arts and Crafts Movement appeared at the same time as Karl Marx's socialism. Both were, in part, reactions to the Industrial Revolution with its 'dark, satanic mills' and grinding poverty.

Early Arts and Crafts ideas were shaped by two key design principles. The first was a desire for the 'truthful' use of materials – the idea that every part of a house design should perform a straightforward and transparent function, and that the materials should be natural, hand-crafted and high quality. Features that appeared to be structural but were in fact cosmetic, such as false timber beams and stuck-on columns, were shunned. The second principle was a wholesale rejection of industrialization, which manifested itself in a desire to capture the beauty of nature in decorative details. Birds, flowers, leaves, vines, animals and fruit – all these became common motifs in Arts and Crafts decoration.

These key principles were brought to life in the design and building of Red House in 1859. Designed by the architect Philip Webb, Red House was to be the private home of the newly married William Morris. This house,

revolutionary for its time, encapsulated the emerging style. It was conceived from the inside out – the windows and doors sized and located to suit the function of the room, rather than adhering to an imposed exterior design. The exterior of the house was built from local red brick and tiles, chosen for their variation and character. Webb did not try to hide these simple materials, as was typically the case in house building of this time. On the contrary, he celebrated and drew attention to them.

While the exterior and floor plan were Webb's design, the rich interiors were all Morris's work: the theatrical wooden staircase with newel posts like chess pieces, the beautiful stained glass, the exposed timber structure and the large, specially designed wooden furniture. The exquisite wallpaper that Morris designed to decorate the ceiling panels was sparingly used, allowing space to breathe, and the walls were surprisingly bare. The floor in the entrance hall was covered with simple quarry tiles, and the fireplaces made from red bricks, both of which echoed the exterior of the building.

Morris went on to dominate the decorative arts throughout the late Victorian period and continued his passion for medieval architecture by founding the Society for the Protection of Ancient Buildings (SPAB), which has done so much to save the buildings he idealized. By contrast, Webb's retiring nature and refusal to have any of his building plans published meant that it was down to other architects, such as Richard Norman Shaw, to bring Arts and Crafts architecture to the fore.

Shaw developed a style called 'Old English', which blended half-timbering, hung tiles, stone mullioned windows and tall decorative chimneys. It was a mishmash of design influences, both English and Dutch, and captured the imaginations of an emerging generation of architects. This new generation spread the ideas of Arts and Crafts and ensured that Britain was at the frontline of design in the late nineteenth century.

The doorway, *far left*, and drawing room settle, *left*, at Red House show the simple, well-proportioned, well-made ideals of the Arts and Crafts Movement.

RIGHT Arts and Crafts architect Charles Voysey's childlike houses struck a chord with people at odds with the rapid pace of change in the late nineteenth century.

Paradoxically this cutting-edge 'Old English' style was used by Shaw to build some of the first suburbs at the start of the twentieth century – a daring and radical design idea that has since become a symbol of conservatism.

The Arts and Crafts movement is, in fact, full of such contradictions. Despite noble socialist intentions, its original clients were largely from the wealthy upper middle classes. This paradox dogged Morris, a fierce socialist, throughout his life. The dream of craftsmen freely expressing themselves through the act of building fell somewhat flat when it was actually the architects who were designing everything down to the last door handle. A movement that started with the 'truthful' use of materials as a key principle later inspired the stick-on half-timbering and mock Tudor pastiche so prevalent in latter-day suburbia.

There was even a tension between the decorative interiors most of us associate with Arts and Crafts and the desire to re-create the simplicity of the medieval interiors that first captured Morris's imagination. The work of Charles Voysey, whose charming, almost childlike houses are synonymous with the movement, sums up this conflict. He was one of the most successful wallpaper designers at the turn of the twentieth century, but felt that wallpaper should be used only because 'most modern furniture is vulgar or bad in every way, elaborate papers of many colours help to disguise its ugliness'. Given a choice, Voysey preferred simple oak furniture, plain carpets and whitewashed walls with little decoration. Oddly, he used wallpaper in his own house, so one can only assume that he didn't like even his own furniture!

Despite these contradictions, the Arts and Crafts Movement had at its core a set of values that inspired an extraordinary range of brilliant graphic design, decorative arts and buildings around the world. It is these principles that should be the guide for anyone restoring an Arts and Crafts building: truthful use of materials, simplicity, good workmanship and naturally inspired design.

INTERIORS

Few historic houses have their original interior design schemes left intact. For many buildings, this isn't a problem – it's only natural that wallpapers, paint colours and furniture styles should move with the times. However, if you've spent a long time restoring an old house to its former glory, you may feel reluctant to fill it with modern designs, fixtures and fittings.

Getting the right balance between high-tech conveniences and period charm isn't always easy; a truly authentic Victorian kitchen, for example, would be unworkable for most modern families. Some people go for an eclectic approach, picking bits from their favourite periods and putting them together in one design scheme. Others go for the best that modern design has to offer, or, conversely, try to re-create as closely as possible the authentic period style of their building. The choice is yours.

If you do want to restore the interior of your historic house to its old self, this chapter offers a brief overview of the various period styles and how to go about re-creating them. Bear in mind that unless you have documented or physical evidence for the original design scheme of your home, you can re-create only a general sense of what it must have been like rather than achieve a truly accurate representation. It's also worth knowing that interior fashions always took a while to spread from the wealthier sections of society to everyday homes, and that London and other big cities were often years ahead of smaller towns and villages in terms of new designs and materials.

Historic wallpapers and fabrics rarely survive, but where they do, they offer a fantastic insight into interiors of the past.

That said, you can still have a pretty good stab at re-creating an authentic historic interior from scratch. There are lots of great resources available to help a house restorer find out more about domestic design

The increasing availability of glass towards the end of the sixteenth century led to lighter, brighter interiors, as seen here in the hall at Little Moreton Hall in Cheshire.

from the past. One particularly good source is the Geffrye Museum in east London, which has a series of rooms decorated to show the development of interiors over the centuries. There are also two essential reference books that offer a comprehensive look at the subject: *The Elements of Style: An Encyclopedia of Domestic Architectural Detail* edited by Stephen Calloway, and *Authentic Décor: The Domestic Interior 1620–1920* by Peter Thornton (see page 252). Now on to the different periods...

TUDOR AND JACOBEAN STYLE (1485–1625)

The end of the fifteenth century is a good place to start an overview of the English interior – not because houses before this date lacked any type of recognizable decor, but because their rarity renders it difficult to make generalizations about the interiors. Also, the late fifteenth century is probably the earliest the average house restorer will have to go back because most buildings constructed before this time are not in private hands.

So what were the major developments? Prior to the Tudor period, in medieval times, the hearth would have been in the centre of the room, with smoke billowing up through a hole in the ceiling. After the fireplace was moved to one wall it became an important decorative focal point for the first time. In expensive houses, overmantels (which occupy the space above a fireplace) were commonly adorned with coats of arms and heraldic figures, while the fireplaces themselves were often spanned by a simple gently pointed arch. Ceilings, now free of smoke and dirt from the hearth, could become a focus for pattern and decorative plasterwork, often in the

form of grids or 'strapwork' (see below). The increasing availability of glass also had an effect on interiors during this time, especially towards the end of the sixteenth century and beginning of the seventeenth. Lighter, brighter rooms gave home-owners the incentive to decorate their interiors more elaborately, as much of this detail would previously have been lost in poor light conditions.

Italy made a big impression on English designers of the day. The Renaissance was in full swing by the fifteenth century, and classical motifs from both ancient Greece and Rome made their presence known. These included carved acanthus leaves and scrolls, as well as columns, pillars, porticoes and rounded arches. Classical proportions were key, and mathematics brought symmetry and order to both building design and interior décor.

But Italy wasn't the only country to exert its influence over early English interiors. From 1560 books that described exciting new design details began to flood into the country from the Netherlands, and many were a hit among the upper echelons of society. Strapwork was one of the popular motifs in these books, and was widely adopted for use on ceilings, fireplaces and woodwork. Originating in Antwerp, it was essentially a pattern formed by interlacing strips, either painted or carved on stone, wood or plaster. Other typical designs from this period include 'linenfold' – an effect carved into wood panelling to make it look like folds of fabric – and carved leaf patterns.

Hardwood, particularly oak, was popular for both doors and ornately carved wall panelling in affluent homes, although most houses would have

Shakespeare's birthplace in Stratford-upon-Avon provides a fascinating glimpse into a typical Elizabethan interior. Painted cloths can be seen on the walls.

made do with lime-plastered and limewashed walls. In the smarter houses, half-panelled walls were often topped with sumptuous tapestries or painted cloths, but wallpaper was still a rarity. Underfoot, stone slabs covered the ground floor, and wide oak or elm boards furnished the upper storeys. Woven rush matting was employed as an early version of carpeting, while oriental rugs were a rare indulgence, seen only in the richest residences. Such was the cost of imported rugs that they were considered too nice to walk on, and were used instead underneath the best pieces of furniture in the house or as table coverings.

BAROQUE STYLE (1625–1714)

Moving away from the Jacobean and into the Baroque era, classical motifs and proportions continued to be important in interior design. Architects of the day, however, reinterpreted them in fresh and exciting ways. This new movement, which again started in Italy, wanted to get away from some of the more sombre aspects of Renaissance interiors and move instead towards a wonderfully flamboyant and indulgent design palate. All the traditional elements of classical architecture were there – arches, columns, pediments – but Baroque designers embellished them with extravagant carved designs and rich patterns. The mood was one of opulence and splendour. Popular motifs of the day included cupids, angels, swags, fruit and flowers, all executed in a naturalistic way, and every surface had to be decorated, from ceilings and walls to furniture and floor coverings. Far from being 'less is more', it was definitely 'more is more'.

ABOVE Exaggerated versions of classical forms, such as cherubs, were distinctive features of Baroque.

LEFT Many mid-Georgian rooms successfully combined classical details with more flamboyant touches.

In wealthy homes walls were often covered with intricately carved oak, walnut or cheaper pine panelling (pine becoming more commonly used in response to dwindling supplies of native hardwood). Stencilling was a popular way of decorating softwood panelling, or it was sometimes painted to look like an expensive material, such as marble or oak. Where half-height panelling was used, the upper sections of the walls were often covered with patterned leather panels, luxurious textiles or handmade tapestries. Uncovered walls might be lime-plastered and limewashed, then stencilled or decorated with *trompe l'oeil* illusions. *Trompe l'oeil* decorations were also used to great effect on ceilings, as were allegorical paintings and scenes from classical history. Roof interiors were decorated with elaborate plasterwork and decorative cornicing, although modest homes would be limited to plain plaster ceilings. Wallpaper was still extremely rare, although hand-blocked papers began to emerge in small numbers.

At the beginning of the Baroque period curtains were a rare luxury, although simple blinds in plain white or cream fabrics were common from the mid-seventeenth century; only at the end of the century did they become a regular feature in wealthier houses, most often in the form of paired or pull-up curtains. Favourite fabrics during this period were silk damask and velvet, but chintz (patterned cotton with a glazed finish) also appeared for the first time. At the heart of the room, fireplaces were also enjoying the Baroque treatment; overmantels displayed exaggerated versions of the classical elements and naturalistic forms of earlier periods, and would often include an inset mirror panel, a forerunner to today's overmantel mirror.

The interiors at Kelmarsh Hall, a red-brick Georgian country house in Northamptonshire, where eighteenth-century chic meets 1920s glamour.

On the floors, stone was a popular choice, as were bricks and tiles. Oak was still being used for the upstairs floors, but in many houses softwood boards or lime plaster applied on wooden laths were successful alternatives. If budget permitted, marble was a popular choice, especially laid in complicated black and white patterns, while parquet flooring made its first appearance in the wealthiest homes. Rush matting continued to be a useful floor covering, and brightly coloured British copies of Turkish carpets, known as 'turkeywork', began to emerge. The extensive use of coloured marble, gilding, blue and white ceramics, lacquerwork, giltwood furniture and mirrors were also key features of this period.

PALLADIAN AND NEO-CLASSICAL STYLE (1714–1811)

Soon after George I came to the throne in 1714, the 3rd Earl of Burlington, an influential patron of the arts, led a campaign to rid the country of what he saw as the indiscipline and excesses of the Baroque period. Repulsed by the over-ornate and hedonistic design schemes of Baroque architects, he wanted to reinstate a pure, classical architectural style based on the forms and philosophy of sixteenth-century architect Andrea Palladio (who himself was inspired by the teachings of ancient Roman architect Marcus Vitruvius Pollio).

Burlington's mission was a success, and for almost half a century Palladian interiors were the height of fashion. Sombre, bold and dignified in tone, these early Georgian rooms were heavily architectural in style, filled with huge Roman columns, pediments (triangular shapes often used above doors) and pilasters (flat rectangular columns fixed against a wall).

ABOVE RIGHT Roman ornaments and chinoiserie – two favourites of the Neo-Classical interior designer.

LEFT A typical 1750s Georgian drawing room from Hatchlands in Surrey.

Roman sculpted motifs were common, including female figures, busts on columns, and masks, but above all else proportion was the key to the Palladian style: the proportions of windows to wall space, of ceiling height to room length, of door to roof height and so on. The dimensions had to be mathematically precise, so to help out nervous builders and home-owners, guides and pattern books, such as James Gibbs's *Book of Architecture* (1728), set out in fine detail the exact measurements and elements of a typical Palladian home. By the middle of the eighteenth century, however, Palladian ideals were starting to feel a little too prescriptive and humourless. There simply wasn't enough room for individuality. A number of new intermediate styles emerged at this stage and filled the void perfectly, two of the best known being Rococo and Gothick.

Rococo was characterized by lighthearted and witty design themes. The style had already been a hit across Europe, especially in France, and was expressed in the lavish use of fanciful motifs, such as scrolls, scallops, shells, rocks, animals and plant forms. Some people, however, found Rococo a little too wild for their taste. In 1737, in his book *De la Distribution des Maisons de Plaisance* (The Arrangement of Country Houses), architecture professor François Blondel criticized the Rococo style as a 'ridiculous jumble of shells, dragons, reeds, palm-trees, and plants'.

While the Rococo style never really took hold in Britain, Gothick designs held a wider appeal for the Georgians. Based on romantic notions about the medieval period, Gothick interiors borrowed heavily from true Gothic architecture of the twelfth to sixteenth centuries but had little to do with historical accuracy. Exaggerated and over-romantic, Gothick rooms

contained all the familiar elements of medieval Gothic architecture such as pointed arches, foils (leaf-shaped curves), gargoyles and heraldic emblems applied with reckless abandon. Mock ruins and follies were the order of the day in the gardens of stately homes, whilst many buildings, including Horace Walpole's now famous Strawberry Hill house in London, were given entire fairy-tale Gothick 'makeovers', complete with medieval-style battlements and stained-glass windows. (Gothick later matured into the more familiar and widespread Gothic Revival style of the early nineteenth century, which was far more historically accurate and is best represented by the Houses of Parliament built in 1836.)

Pointed arches, quatrefoils and heraldic emblems were popular motifs of the Gothic Revival movement.

Despite the refreshing daftness of both Rococo and Gothick styles, the Georgians could never truly tear themselves away from the pull of classical architecture. For the latter half of the eighteenth century Neo-Classicism was the prevailing architectural fashion. Similar in ideals and tone to the Palladian movement, Neo-Classicism still looked back to ancient Rome for its inspiration, but was much lighter and more elegant and refined in its application. The focus moved away from heavy architectural components and concentrated instead on smaller decorative details, such as plasterwork and wallpapers. Neo-Classicism is also known as 'Adam style', after one of the main proponents of the movement, architect Robert Adam (and to a lesser extent his brothers James and John Adam).

Neo-Classical architects were very keen on classical imagery and ornament, inspired by the wealth of new information that was pouring out of archaeological excavations in places such as Pompeii and Herculaneum. Ceilings in well-to-do houses were often the main focal point, and

decorated with beautifully executed floral and leaf motifs copied from classical sources. In some of the finest houses, glorious plaster ceilings were also embellished with painted scenes from Greek or Roman mythology. Other common motifs included acanthus leaves, urns and vases, animal heads, fruit and floral garlands, rosettes and husks (stylized buds). Any raised plaster or carved ornament was often picked out with gilt for extra effect, and sections of the ceiling were frequently painted in different tones of the same colour. Common ceiling colours included light green, lilac, apricot, pink and terracotta.

Mirrors became really important during this period. Robert Adam would plan the mirrors for a room scheme with as much care and attention to detail as the ceiling. Tall mirror panels would reflect light back into the room, creating the illusion of space, and would often be placed behind gilded candlebras or girandoles (wall-mounted candlebras) to magnify the candlelight. Mirrors were also used to great effect above fireplaces, behind console tables and between pairs of sash windows.

Stone-flagged floors remained popular, especially in the entrance halls of large houses, but wood was becoming the most common material on the lower and upper floors. Hardwood was used in the most prestigious rooms, but it was also acceptable to have pine or fir. These softwood floors were almost always stained and polished, then covered with a large rug, whether an expensive import from France or the Orient, or a cheaper British copy. During the Neo-Classical period the carpet industry began to emerge. Although still expensive, wall-to-wall carpets with classical motifs or pretty floral patterns could be found in many of the larger houses.

Mirrors and statues were used to great effect in Neo-Classical interiors, such as this one at Attingham Park in Shropshire.

Part of the lighter feel of Neo-Classical interiors comes from the treatment of walls. Palladian rooms were often panelled from floor to ceiling with dark, heavy woods, or painted in dull, muted colours, such as sage green, grey-blue and brown. By contrast, during the Neo-Classical period wall panelling often reached only chair height, with the upper portion of the wall painted in fresh, airy colours, such as light green, primrose, sky blue, Wedgwood blue, dusky pink or off-white.

When panelling wasn't used at all, which became increasingly common as the Neo-Classical period wore on, a simple dado rail would divide the wall, the lower portion being painted in white or stone and the upper portion being either painted or covered in wallpaper. Popular wallpaper designs from this period included Neo-Classical motifs, such as swags and urns, sometimes applied in flock (powdered wool), and two-colour stripes. Hand-painted Chinese papers, or the English version called 'chinoiserie', were also fashionable.

ABOVE Mass production brought new ideas, such as indoor bathrooms and decorative tiles, within the reach of the Victorian middle class.

RIGHT Over-stuffed upholstery, elaborate lace and numerous nick-nacks characterized the Victorian parlour.

VICTORIAN STYLE (1837–1901)

The Victorian era saw huge changes in interior design. The rise of mass production allowed a newly emerging middle class to indulge itself in domestic design and fashionable furnishings in a way never previously possible. Huge exhibitions showcased the latest and greatest in household products, from gas-fired kitchen stoves to knife-sharpening machines, while increased foreign trade encouraged a passion for all things exotic, including African, Indian and Chinese designs. Even new industrial

processes, such as lamination and electroplating, meant that a whole new raft of household items could be bought and displayed with pride.

In fact, given the diversity of the period, it is difficult to pin down a style that is definitively Victorian. It was a time of imitation and reinterpretation of previous stylistic eras, while also cherry-picking all the best bits of world culture. It is not unusual to find a Victorian house with a Gothic Revival library, a Neo-Classical-style entrance hall, and oriental or Moorish designs dotted around the walls. Factories could also produce cheap reproductions of previously expensive interior features, such as

Towards the end of the Victorian period, room schemes became less cluttered and more restrained in style, as seen here in the pioneeringly modern Cragside House in Northumberland.

decorative plasterwork or wallpaper, so even the most modest of middle-class homes would have a wealth of interesting period details. Home-owners were quite happy to combine more than one style in the same room, so Persian rugs would sit comfortably with Chinese-style wallpapers, classical-inspired fabrics and a Renaissance-style fireplace.

Despite this eclectic approach to interior design, there are common features to Victorian room schemes. Perhaps most obvious is the love of clutter. Rooms were stuffed full of furniture, fabrics, ornaments, lighting, cushions, side-tables, mirrors, plants and anything else that socially ambitious people could get their hands on. In fact, the Victorians loved collecting and displaying bric-a-brac so much that the size of the average mantelpiece significantly increased during the nineteenth century. 'Whatnots' also appeared at this time. These were tiered wooden stands for displaying knick-knacks. Typical ornaments included candlesticks, stuffed animals in glass jars, porcelain figures, dried flowers and carriage clocks. Every bit of wall space would be covered with framed paintings and prints: dramatic landscapes, scenes from mythology or the Bible, sporting subjects, portraits and delicate watercolours were all popular. Tapestries and samplers (often showing a moral or religious quotation) were also favourites, especially ones made by members of the household.

The walls themselves would often be covered in highly patterned wallpaper above the dado rail, with painted Anaglypta (a make of embossed paper) below. Paint effects were popular, especially faux marbling or graining of cheap softwoods, stencilling and stippling. In the middle of the nineteenth century wallpaper went into mass production,

Slender columns, carved in the shape of long-stemmed flowers, from the White Drawing Room at Blackwell Arts and Crafts house in Bowness-on-Windermere.

allowing for a huge proliferation of designs and finishes. Favourite patterns included large flowers, such as dahlias and hydrangeas, as well as realistic representations of birds and animals. With the Arts and Crafts Movement, which emerged in the 1860s, came the introduction of William Morris wallpapers, which featured beautifully stylized floral and medieval repeating patterns. You can still pick up Morris & Co designs from wallpaper manufacturer Sanderson, who purchased the company's entire collection of wallpaper printing blocks and colour records back in 1927. Sanderson also acquired a collection of Morris printed fabrics at the same time, which would be perfect for re-creating the textiles of a mid- or late-Victorian room. You could also use heavier fabrics, such as velvet and damask, for downstairs curtains (plus lace nets), with cottons and chintz for the bedrooms. Trimmings, in the form of tassels, braids and ribbons, were at their height during this time. Fabrics were even draped over the mantelpiece, but this constitutes a major fire hazard if you plan to use the grate, so is probably best avoided.

On the floors there would have been wall-to-wall carpets, or large rugs surrounded by a band of polished or stained wooden floor. Patterns were mostly dark and heavy, often with blowzy floral designs or geometric patterns. Oriental and Turkish designs were also great favourites. In the bedrooms and attics rag rugs or small floorcloths (canvas painted with oils) were popular, while halls and kitchen floors were often covered with intricately patterned encaustic tiles. (Making the tiles involved a caustic process, whereby coloured pigments and hot wax were burnt into the surface.) Many of these encaustic floors are still intact and worth

Naturalistic motifs, such as flowers, animals and berries, dominated Arts and Crafts decoration, especially William Morris's wallpaper and fabrics.

preserving at all costs. You could expect to pay around £600 per square metre for reclaimed Minton replacements.

No Victorian ceiling was complete without a plaster ceiling rose, a feature that has unfortunately been ripped out of many period homes. Luckily, you can get replacement decorative plaster roses and pieces of missing mouldings and cornicing from any number of firms; look in Yellow Pages for a company near you. Failing that, try the Building Conservation Directory (see page 246). Ceilings were mostly painted in off-white, although patterned wallpapers and paint effects were sometimes used to create an even more opulent look.

The only word for Victorian upholstered furniture is overstuffed. Look out for deep, plump armchairs and sofas. Ottomans (footstools or seats without back or arms), chaises longues and pouffes were also common, with many examples often crammed into one room. At the beginning of the Victorian period most wooden furniture was crafted from mahogany, but as the century wore on, lighter woods, such as satinwood, also became common. Gothic Revival furniture and Arts and Crafts pieces were often made from oak, a favourite material of the medieval period. On the whole, Victorian furniture was heavy and dark, with large dining tables, sideboards, bureaux, balloon-back chairs and display cabinets being popular items. Upstairs, however, cheaper painted pine was often employed for bedroom furniture, such as blanket-boxes, bedside tables and chests of drawers. Ironically, these less prestigious pieces of furniture are often more collectable and desirable in today's antique market than the dark brown woods.

LEFT Hampstead Garden Suburb – the epitome of suburban style.

RIGHT Tree-lined roads and open green spaces provided an alternative to the dirty, unhealthy cities of yesteryear.

A HEALTHY LIFE IN THE GARDEN SUBURB (1890–1920)

The Industrial Revolution had, by and large, been a grubby affair. By the middle of the nineteenth century, overcrowding was endemic and all the major towns and cities in Britain suffered from polluted freshwater supplies and overflowing sewage. Typhoid, cholera, diarrhoea and dysentery were rife, even among the upper classes. The pressing problems of poor housing and sanitation had to be tackled.

In 1875 a ground-breaking Public Health Act required all local authorities to abide by building regulations or 'bye-laws'. These dictated that every new house should have its own sanitation and water supply. Long rows of well-spaced terrace housing were constructed, known as bye-law houses, which, combined with a huge programme of public sewer building, led to an immediate and welcome improvement in urban health.

But despite the positive benefits of bye-law housing, by the end of the century it had come under attack for being too monotonous. Architects and social reformers of the day called for a more imaginative approach to the problem of unhealthy housing. The Victorian obsession with clean air and a nostalgia for the countryside combined with the need for urban housing to create one of Britain's most prominent architectural contributions to the world – the 'garden suburb'.

During the 1870s Bedford Park in west London became the prototype for later garden suburbs and was hugely influential as a concept for new housing developments. Spacious semi-detached and detached houses of varying and individual design were built amongst leafy, irregular roads. Parks and community facilities created a warm, welcoming atmosphere and encouraged a feeling of being connected to nature, a key theme from the Arts and Crafts era. Designed by Richard Norman Shaw, himself a prominent architect in the Arts and Crafts Movement, the Bedford Park scheme was built in the 'Old English' style. Large, Tudor-inspired, multi-paned windows and generous floor plans cultivated an interior feel known as 'Sweetness and Light'. It was a style desirable to many suburbanites as a reaction

LEFT An Arts and Crafts-inspired house in Hampstead Garden Suburb.

RIGHT Informal, light and spacious interiors: the Edwardians aspired to a totally different lifestyle from their formal Victorian parents.

to the dark, gloomy homes of their parents that were often dominated by small rooms, clutter and narrow corridors. The new style also opened itself out to the world, with balconies, large windows and a new emphasis on the garden.

The ideas from Bedford Park were consolidated and set down in a manifesto in 1898 by Ebenezer Howard. In *Tomorrow: A Peaceful Path to Real Reform* he put together a plan that combined his own experiences of urban and rural life with ideas from leading philanthropists of the day, such as John Ruskin and William Morris. (Morris had long campaigned for the concept of 'decency of surroundings ... ample space, well-built, clean healthy housing [and] abundant garden space'.) Howard's manifesto laid out a plan for 'organized urban centres for 32,000 inhabitants, surrounded by a green belt of farms and parks'.

The idea of combining city and country living was immediately successful, and despite the somewhat vague designs set out by Howard, it captured people's imaginations. In 1903 First Garden City Limited bought a tract of land in Letchworth, Hertfordshire, and fleshed out Howard's loose plan to create the first true 'garden suburb'. Laid out using winding roads that responded in harmony to the existing landscape, it created a visually rich environment. Using a friendly, approachable Arts and Crafts-inspired style, the architects established a low housing density that gave each individual home ample sunlight, good views, seclusion and privacy. These ideas were further developed in Hampstead Garden Suburb, begun in 1906, where architects created short, village-like streets and cul-de-sacs that are now synonymous with suburbia.

Inside the home there were equally significant changes. Layouts were designed to reflect a new social climate, one less obsessed with privacy and formality. Some rooms became multi-purpose, and the idea of a room for 'best' was considered less important. There were even experiments with open-plan living.

Technology revolutionized how the garden suburb house actually functioned. Running water became common around

1870 and gas lighting started to appear in 1880. Electric lighting followed in the next decade, and up until 1900, gas and electric battled to become the lighting of choice through intense marketing and advertising campaigns. By the outbreak of World War I in 1914, the ease and cleanliness of electric lighting had triumphed, and it became the norm in most new middle-class housing. The introduction of these lighting technologies also affected decoration styles. It was realized that a pale-coloured room takes significantly less light to illuminate; a room with a white ceiling and cream walls used half the number of candles or electric lights than a room with dark panels.

Heating was still provided by open fires and ranges, so the hearth remained the central feature in the living room. Using tiles, fake marble, wood or cast iron, the design of fireplaces became increasingly subject to new trends as magazines and advertising vied for customers. Similarly, fitted furniture like inglenooks, cosy corners and fitted screens allowed proud home-owners to change and customize the look of their houses relatively cheaply in order to keep up with the fast-changing fashions of the day.

It does seem extraordinary now however that, despite all these advances, by 1904 it was still rare to find a lavatory in the house. There were baths and even showers in dedicated bathrooms but one still had to go outside to answer the call of nature. In spite of this, at the start of the twentieth century British housing had become the most advanced in the world. Just as the sun was setting on the British Empire and the world of Edwardian splendour was torn apart by the carnage of World War I, there was, for a brief period, a 'golden age' in housing, one that established the ideas and styles that still dominate the way many of us live today.

PERIOD GARDENS

If you want to restore a historic garden, you're up against a few challenges. The first is that often very little remains of the original – perhaps only a flavour or impression of the layout. Gardens also evolve and change over time. While this is one of their greatest assets, it can make it difficult to keep your garden faithful to any one period in time. Old plants die, new ones pop up. Rarely is it possible to keep a firm grip on the entire scheme, unless you're an experienced gardener with lots of time, energy and resources available. Finally, unlike buildings, gardens take time to grow and mature. Your house restoration project might be finished in a year, but the garden could take ten or fifteen years to reach glorious maturity.

Still, that doesn't mean you shouldn't have a crack at attempting to restore a historic garden, or create an entirely new one from scratch. There's nothing more satisfying than a garden that sits comfortably with a house: it's a marriage made in heaven, and one that will not only enhance the experience of living in a period home, but will actually add value to your property as well.

So what's the best way to approach restoring a garden? The first rule is to be relaxed. Don't worry if it's going to take years to mature. Don't worry if you can't get hold of all the authentic plants. And, above all, don't worry if you can't afford all the landscaping, engineering and garden features that a period garden might require. A suggestion of the past will be just as enjoyable as something that's strictly historically accurate.

This chapter provides a potted history of the different types of garden from each period, with common plants, layouts and designs. If you do own

From rambling wild flowers, *left*, to classical follies, *above right*, period gardens are as varied as their accompanying houses.

a historically significant garden or a large plot in need of serious tender loving care, it's almost certainly better to get the professionals on board. The Garden History Society (see page 247) is a great place to start your search for a qualified gardener, and if you join up as a member, you can draw on the expertise available within the society to develop your own knowledge and understanding of gardens and garden history. If you're in a hurry, however, you'll find quick hints and tips at the History of British Gardening link on the BBC's website (see page 245).

RESTORING GARDENS

The Victorians were the first generation to try to restore historic gardens with any consistency. Their passion for history and archaeology, combined with their love of plants and ornaments, meant that they often tried very hard to get it right. Unfortunately, trying hard doesn't always work. Gardens renovated during this period often have an over-restored feel to them: for example, the arms and legs were often replaced on ancient Roman garden statues.

In modern times historic garden restoration is a little more circumspect. The National Trust, for example, has the philosophy that the garden of an ancient house should reflect the diversity of styles that the property has undergone, especially if it has been lived in and adapted over many generations. A fine example of this approach is at Newby Hall, near Ripon in Yorkshire. The garden lies between the house and the river Ure, and was originally constructed by Peter Aram, an exceptional gardener, at

Tree- and hedge-lined avenues direct the eye towards Newby Hall in North Yorkshire.

the end of the seventeenth century. The garden was laid out in the form of a *patte d'oie* (goose foot) – three long avenues with the features arranged between them. These included an orchard, a huge parterre (a level area containing beds surrounded by clipped hedges), rows of trees, flower-beds, pots and statues, with fine gravel in between. This basic shape, despite many changes to the house and the land over the last 300 years, is still tangible today, although little remains of the original planting. What matters is that the essence of the garden endures.

To create something on a more domestic scale, the present-day restorer might wish to have a garden that complements the style and proportions of the house, concentrating on the essential period elements without becoming obsessive about detail. Making the most of existing features – original trees, period structures, walkways and paths – will help you to do this, as will picking out a few of the appropriate historic plants and ornaments.

PERIOD GARDEN STYLES

Little is known about the extent to which gardens were 'designed' in England prior to the sixteenth century. Before that time, gardening was primarily a means to an end – to provide vegetables, fruit, herbs, medicinal plants and, occasionally, a sheltered place for sitting. There are early references to gardening, though: a medieval window in Canterbury Cathedral (twelfth century) shows Adam delving into a garden with a spade and mattock, for example, while *De Naturis Rerum* (On the Nature of Things) by Alexander Neckham, published in 1190, listed 200 garden

Two classics of British garden design – climbing roses at Mottisfont Abbey, Hampshire, *left*, and formal topiary at Lytes Cary Manor, Somerset, *above*.

plants, some of which were encountered during the Crusades. It also contains the earliest known reference to a wheelbarrow.

So what else do we know about early gardens? By 1340 the herb rosemary was introduced into Britain from Antwerp, and in some aristocratic gardens from this time there was ornamental topiary. From archaeology and written sources we can glean that monasteries and castles often had a small garden close to the walls, filled with medicinal and culinary herbs. Plants grew in square or rectangular beds that were often raised and edged with planks. Trellis or wattle fences were also used. Rose-covered arbours were a common feature, but in general only a very limited range of plants was grown – perhaps 250 types in total, including fruit and vegetables, and over half being native British species. A 1440 publication, *The Feate of Gardening*, mentions chamomile, cornflowers, coriander, cowslip, fennel, St John's wort, lavender, rue and valerian. Just to give you a comparison, by 1841 there were over 1200 varieties of dahlia alone.

The sixteenth-century garden

Henry VIII was a keen garden lover, but his Dissolution of the Monasteries (1536–40) after splitting with Rome was disastrous not just for the buildings, but for their grounds too. Many of the monks' carefully tended herbal gardens, orchards and vineyards were lost forever. However, domestic gardeners of the early Tudor period continued growing herbs and vegetables. Raised beds, paths and arbours were enclosed within low hedges or fences of trellis, and shady alleys were covered in vines. The few decorative plants from this time (roses, marigolds and rosemary, for example) were always useful, as well as aesthetically pleasing. Tudor town houses sometimes had gardens, but these were generally modest and functional, growing just a few plants, such as clary sage and thyme, for medicinal, culinary and household use. A fantastic example of this type of garden can be seen at the Geffrye Museum in east London (see page 247).

A fountain in the Rose Garden at Nymans Garden, West Sussex.

Towards the end of the Tudor period the Renaissance style of gardening, imported from Europe, began to trickle into wealthy gardens, bringing with it classical statues and knot gardens (low hedges worked into intricate patterns, with sand, gravel or plants in the spaces). Unlike gardens of today, many Renaissance gardens were built to be enjoyed from above, specifically the upper floors of a grand house. Little Moreton Hall in Cheshire has a reconstructed knot garden that can be viewed in this way.

The seventeenth-century garden

By the beginning of the seventeenth century there was a new emphasis on gardens as places of pure enjoyment. In 1618 William Lawson published *The Country Housewife's Garden* and *A New Orchard and Garden*, both specifically aimed at women, which talked about the recreational and sensual delights of gardening. He describes an ornamental orchard divided into squares, with a small knot at each corner – a design to give pleasure as well as fruit. A natural progression from this idea was the notion of growing flowers simply for their beauty. Gardens could also be places of fun and folly: under the influence of French designers, royal and noble gardens often made use of decorative water features and grottos. The 1627 grotto at Woburn Abbey still survives today.

ABOVE LEFT Tulip mania reached its peak in the 1630s.

RIGHT The walled garden at Helmingham Hall in Suffolk.

Knowledge about different plants was also increasing apace. In 1621 the first botanical garden was set up at Oxford University (you can still visit it today), and in 1629 John Parkinson's punningly titled *Paradisi in Sole Paradisus Terrestris* (Park-in-Sun's Earthly Paradise) described over 1000 different garden plants, as well as offering expert advice on the joys of fruit-tree cultivation and aromatic gardens. John Tradescant the Elder, royal gardener to Charles I, recorded rare plants as fascinating curiosities during the seventeenth century. He travelled widely in Europe and North Africa, and brought exciting new species, such as spiderwort and Virginia creeper, back to Britain.

Wealthy families were keen to make the most of these fashionable floral finds and to show off their new-found gardening expertise. Hatfield House in Hertfordshire, for example, had one of the greatest plant collections in Europe at this time. Varieties of quince, medlar, pear, apple, currant, apricot, peach, nectarine, pomegranate, orange and cherry were all cultivated there, along with flowers such as pinks and anemones. The owners of Hatfield also experimented with early hydraulic engineering, building a pumping-house that provided the garden with a small river, fountains and pools. Ornamental canals also became popular.

Plant collecting became very fashionable among the well-off. While the tulip, a native Asian plant, had been in Europe since 1572, it didn't reach its height of popularity until the 1630s. The resulting 'tulip mania' saw people paying extraordinary sums of money for new varieties and rare colours of tulip; by 1676 there were at least 200 varieties known to exist in Britain alone. Early flower and bulb collectors of this time were known as

Gothic follies, and classical temples made attractive and dramatic focal points on eighteenth-century estates, such as Stowe in Buckinghamshire, *left*, and Stourhead in Wiltshire, *right*.

'florists', and tended to collect species such as carnations, anemones, ranunculus and auriculus. Individual and expensive specimen plants were often displayed separately in pots or beds to show off a gardener's plantsmanship to full effect. Other commonly grown plants in pots from this era include orange, lemon, myrtle and oleander.

The eighteenth-century garden

The eighteenth century was an era dominated by the English Landscape Movement, with Lancelot 'Capability' Brown as its master. Visiting Continental gardens had become a pastime for the young elite undertaking a cultural 'Grand Tour' of Europe as part of their education. After seeing the overgrown, romantic ruins of ancient Greece and Rome, many landowners came home to England hoping to create a 'classical wilderness' look in their own estates. Parks were laid out by Capability Brown with undulating grassland, trees and large ponds, and views of the countryside beyond, with clumps of trees placed strategically to create vistas or emphasize open spaces. Man-made lakes with ornamental bridges and cascades made attractive focal points, as did classical temples, monuments and statues. Beech, oak, Scots pine and sweet chestnut trees were planted to finish the wild woodland effect. Sometimes whole villages were moved to other areas to facilitate the sweeping, 'natural' landscapes. Even fences weren't allowed to ruin the view: this period saw the widespread use of 'ha-has' – deep ditches – which confined livestock to a particular field without the need for stone walling or wooden fencing.

Away from royal and aristocratic estates, flower gardening continued with enthusiasm, helped along by the wide range of plants and seeds available to the amateur. Large houses in the countryside would have walled flower gardens with formal beds, and separate kitchen gardens for fruit and vegetables. Town gardens, on the other hand, were seen as extensions of the house – places for recreation and entertainment. The introduction of French windows during this period made passing from the house to the garden a natural movement on warm, sunny days. The prevailing taste in these gardens was for simplicity and tidiness, with paved or rolled gravel paths, and geometric beds with box hedging and roses or evergreen shrubs.

The academic study of plants was progressing with great speed. In 1730 William Kent began plans for Kew Gardens, and in 1735 Carolus Linnaeus developed a system for scientifically classifying plants, which is still in use today. Explorers overseas also discovered new species. In 1768 the botanist Joseph Banks sailed to the South Seas with Captain James Cook and brought back specimens of many new plants, and information about their uses. Banks was especially interested in plants that could be used for practical purposes, but he also introduced some of today's favourite ornamentals, including the gardenia, bougainvillea and New Zealand flax.

The eighteenth century was also a great period for garden ornaments and buildings. Roman-style classical temples and Gothick ruins and follies were the order of the day in many estate landscapes. In smaller gardens urns, small statues and ornamental benches were available in Coade stone,

Kitchen gardens, *right*, and dwarf box hedging, *above*, were common in the gardens of large eighteenth-century houses.

The nineteenth century saw a boom in metal garden furniture and glasshouses, thanks to improvements in cast-iron production.

an artificial material that could be moulded and fired (see page 109). Stone plaques, mythical figures and pineapple finials were also common accessories of the day.

The nineteenth-century garden

The Victorians were the ultimate mix-and-matchers. Not only were the interiors of their homes stuffed with features copied from many different eras and cultures, but their gardens received the same eclectic touch. It wasn't uncommon to see Gothic Revival, Baroque and Neo-Classical-style ornaments mixed with Chinese lanterns and bridges, or reproduction artefacts from countries as diverse as France and Japan. In the 1840s Biddulph Grange in Staffordshire, for example, had Chinese, Egyptian and Italian influences in the garden.

The rise of the cast-iron industry led to a boom in metal garden furniture during this century, with the foundries at places such as Coalbrookdale, Carron and Falkirk making huge numbers of cast-iron benches, chairs and tables. Cast iron also made the perfect material for decorative fountains, urns and bird baths.

The Victorian age was also the great era of greenhouses and conservatories. New methods of heating, glass production and cast-iron manufacturing made these structures affordable and popular for the first time, helped along by cutting-edge buildings, such as the Crystal Palace built for the Great Exhibition of 1851. Greenhouses were the perfect environment for raising exotic plants, such as ferns and figs, which were too tender for outside cultivation. Many of these plants were the result of

LEFT The Rose Garden at Sissinghurst, Kent.

RIGHT The advent of the greenhouse allowed the Victorian gardener to grow exotic and unusual plants.

continued world exploration and new hybrid breeding techniques. The dahlia, for instance, having come from Central America originally, was hybridized into every single colour known today by 1818, and less than 25 years later there were over 1000 varieties to choose from. Other significant Victorian plant developments included the discovery and introduction of winter jasmine, camellias, magnolias, Himalayan poppies, azaleas, mahonia, bleeding heart, primulas, windmill palm and skimmia, as well as over 300 species of rhododendron. As for layout, formal gardens were back on the agenda. The Victorians loved the idea of a stepped terrace, adorned with classical urns and vases, linking the house and the garden.

Bedding plants, the brighter the better, became very popular and were laid out in colourful patterns and surrounded by low box hedges. The introduction of the greenhouse allowed the commercial development of bedding favourites, such as geraniums, salvias and lobelia, which could be grown under glass away from frost and pollution damage. The Victorians were also mad about roses, and often created a separate rose garden away from the main plot.

Another great development, this time in the 1830s, was Edwin Budding's invention of the lawnmower. This allowed areas of immaculate lawn to be created in even the most modest of gardens. Prior to this lawns had been the preserve of the rich because it would take three men with scythes a whole day to cut less than half a hectare (1 acre) of grass. By 1858, around 7000 lawnmowers had been sold to domestic gardeners up and down the country.

The cottage garden

The cottage garden – informal, rambling and quintessentially English.

By the end of the Victorian period, home-owners began to tire of the endless formality and bedding plants that had been all the rage in town-house gardens. In their place came a new sense of informality, exemplified in the idea of the English cottage garden – borders filled with herbaceous perennials and huge swathes of harmonizing colours.

The idea of the cottage garden, however, bore little resemblance to the reality of nineteenth-century rural living. Cottage gardens in the countryside were predominantly functional places. Rural workers rarely had the time and inclination to spend hours tending to ornamental flowers; any land attached to their dwellings was generally used for keeping hens, growing herbs and a few vegetables, and possibly keeping beehives. (Honey was an essential sweetening agent, also used in medicines and for preserving food and curing ham.)

The Victorian notion of cottage gardens came instead from the work of William Robinson, whose books described his own style of 'wild' gardening at Gravetye Manor in Sussex, as well as the pretty gardens romanticized in the work of illustrators such as Kate Greenaway, and the writings of Gertrude Jekyll. Now considered to be one of the most influential gardeners of the period, Jekyll had the groundbreaking idea that gardens should be based on colour schemes, not just plants. She also loved the idea of the herbaceous border stuffed with a profusion of flowers, and climbers on trellises and walls. A fine example of her style can be seen at Hestercombe in Somerset, but you can try to re-create your own cottage garden by following her principles (opposite):

- Plant lots of different varieties of small plants close together, leaving no soil showing.
- Mix vegetables and flowers together in the same bed in both front and back garden.
- Have a minimum of lawn, or no lawn at all.
- Make pathways of reclaimed flagstone, old brick or gravel.
- Create areas of interest with wooden or wrought-iron fences, trellises, ponds, bird baths and a garden bench.

HISTORIC GARDENS TO VISIT

One of the best ways to get inspiration and ideas is to have a wander through some of the country's most sensitively restored historic gardens. The UK has some fantastic examples to choose from, and here is just a selection:

Biddulph Grange, near Stoke-on-Trent, Staffordshire
Chatsworth House Gardens, Bakewell, Derbyshire (www.chatsworth-house.co.uk)
Christ Church Cathedral, Oxford (www.chch.ox.ac.uk)
Crathes Castle, near Banchory, Grampian, Scotland
Erdigg, near Wrexham, Clwyd, Wales
Ham House, Petersham, Surrey (www.nationaltrust.org.uk/places/hamhouse)
Hampton Court Palace, East Molesey, Surrey (www.hrp.org.uk)
Hatfield House, Hatfield, Hertfordshire (www.hatfield-house.co.uk)
Hestercombe Gardens, Cheddon Fitzpaine, Taunton, Somerset (www.hestercombegardens.com)
Hidcote, Hidcote Bartrim, Chipping Campden, Gloucestershire (www.nationaltrust.org.uk/hidcote
Little Moreton Hall, Congleton, Cheshire
Mount Stewart, Newtownards, County Down, Northern Ireland
National Botanical Garden of Wales, Llanarthne, Carmarthenshire (www.gardenofwales.org.uk)
National Museum of Gardening, Helston, Cornwall
New Place, Stratford-upon-Avon, Warwickshire
Newby Hall, Ripon, Yorkshire (www.newbyhall.co.uk)
Painswick Rococo Garden, Painswick, near Stroud, Gloucestershire (www.rococogarden.co.uk)
Petworth House, Petworth, West Sussex (www.nationaltrust.org.uk/places/petworth)
RHS Garden, Harlow Carr, Harrogate, Yorkshire
RHS Garden, Wisley, Woking, Surrey
Royal Botanic Gardens, Kew, Richmond, Surrey (www.rbgkew.org.uk)
Queen Eleanor's Garden, Winchester, Hampshire
Rousham, near Steeple Aston, Oxfordshire
St Catherine's College, Oxford (by appointment only)
Tudor House Museum, Bugle Street, Southampton
University Botanic Gardens, Cambridge (www.botanic.cam.ac.uk)
University Botanic Gardens, Oxford (www.botanic-garden.ox.ac.uk)

USEFUL ADDRESSES

ENGLAND

Ancient Monuments Society
St Ann's Vestry
2 Church Entry
London EC4V 5HB
Tel: 020 7236 3934
www.ancientmonumentssociety.org.uk

Dedicated to the study and conservation of ancient monuments, historic buildings and fine old craftsmanship.

Architects Accredited in Building Conservation
see Register of Architects Accredited in Building Conservation

Architectural Heritage Fund
Clareville House
26–27 Oxendon Street
London SW1Y 4EL
Tel: 020 7925 0199
www.ahfund.org.uk

Provides advice, information and financial assistance in the form of grants and low-interest loans for projects undertaken by building preservation trusts (BPTs) and other charities throughout the UK.

Association of Independent Financial Advisers
Austin Friars House
2–6 Austin Friars
London EC2N 2HD
Tel: 020 7628 1287
www.aifa.net

AIFA is the trade association representing Independent Financial Advisers nationwide. The website has a useful 'Find an IFA' search facility.

Association of Preservation Trusts
Clareville House
26–27 Oxendon Street
London SW1Y 4EL
Tel: 020 7930 1629
www.heritage.co.uk/apt

Run under the auspices of the Architectural Heritage Fund, this is the only membership-representative body for building preservation trusts (BPTs) across the UK. Offers members practical advice and support on running a BPT and undertaking building restoration projects.

Bat Conservation Trust
Unit 2, 15 Cloisters House
8 Battersea Park Road
London SW8 4BG
Tel: 020 7627 2629
Fax: 020 7627 2628
Low-call Helpline:
0845 1300 228
Email: enquiries@bats.org.uk
www.bats.org.uk

The Bat Conservation Trust (BCT) is the only national organization solely devoted to bat conservation, and can offer homeowners helpful advice about 'Bats and the Law' should you find your restoration project has uninvited guests!

BBC History of Gardening web pages
www.bbc.co.uk/gardening

Bricks and Brass
2 Aldermary Road
Bromley
Kent BR1 3PH
Tel: 020 8290 1488
www.bricksandbrass.co.uk

Website providing comprehensive information on the architecture, design and history of houses in England, Scotland, Wales and Northern Ireland. Sections cover architectural styles (classical, Gothic, Arts and Crafts, Art Nouveau, etc.), external and internal features (walls, roof, windows, rooms, etc.), period house maintenance and remodelling, and the directory of companies offering products and services, books and events.

British Wood Preserving and Damp-proofing Association
1 Gleneagles House
Vernon Gate
Derby DE1 1UP
Tel: 01332 225100
Fax: 01332 225101
Email: info@bwpda.co.uk
www.bwpda.co.uk

The nationally recognized authority on timber and damp problems. Can help you find a BWPDA-approved specialist in remedial timber treatment and damp-proofing nearest to you.

Building Conservation Directory
www.buildingconservation.com

An online listing of suppliers of products, services and information for the preservation, conservation and restoration of historic buildings, churches and garden landscapes. Also available in book form (see Further Reading).

Carrington Associates
4 Smales Street
York YO1 6EW
Tel: 01904 659544
Mob: 0785 147 9217
Email: carringtonassociates@yahoo.co.uk

Conservation management consultancy. Offers conservation advice and planning guidance for people wanting to restore an historic building. All historic buildings covered, including residential properties, industrial buildings and churches. Covers all areas of the UK.

Churches Conservation Trust
1 West Smithfield
London EC1A 9EE
Tel: 020 7213 0660
www.visitchurches.org.uk

Dedicated to caring for Church of England churches no longer needed for parish use.

Cinema Theatre Association
44 Harrowdene Gardens
Teddington
Middlesex TW11 0DJ
www.cinema-theatre.org.uk

Campaigns for the preservation and continued use of cinemas and theatres, music halls and those entertainment buildings now in use as bingo halls or for other purposes.

Civic Trust
Winchester House
259–269 Old Marylebone Road
London NW1 5RA
Tel: 020 7170 4299
www.civictrust.org.uk

Works with people to promote thriving towns and villages, developing dynamic partnerships between communities, government and business to deliver regeneration and local improvement. Dedicated to bringing vitality and sustainability to the urban environment.

Conservation Register
c/o UK Institute for Conservation
702 The Chandlery
50 Westminster Bridge Road
London SE1 7QY
Tel: 020 7721 8246
www.conservationregister.com

Holds detailed information on conservation-restoration practices from across the UK and Ireland.

Council for British Archaeology
Bowes Morrell House
111 Walmgate
York YO1 9WA
Tel: 01904 671417
www.britarch.ac.uk

Promotes knowledge, appreciation and care of the historic environment for the benefit of present and future generations.

Department for Culture, Media and Sport (DCMS)
2–4 Cockspur Street
London SW1Y 5DH
Tel: 020 7211 6200
www.culture.gov.uk

The DCMS is responsible for government policy on the arts, sport, the national lottery, tourism, libraries, museums and galleries, broadcasting, film, the music industry, press freedom and regulation, licensing, gambling and the historic environment. Also responsible for the listing of historic buildings and scheduling of ancient monuments.

Department for Environment, Food and Rural Affairs
Information Resource Centre
Lower Ground Floor
Ergon House
c/o Nobel House
17 Smith Square
London SW1P 3JR
Tel: 08459 33 55 77
Email at
helpline@defra.gsi.gov.uk
www.defra.gov.uk

DEFRA brings together all aspects of the environment, rural matters, farming and food production and is a focal point for all rural policy, relating to people, the economy and the environment.

Ecology Building Society
7 Belton Road
Silsden
Keighley
West Yorks BD20 0EE
Tel: 0845 674 5566
www.ecology.co.uk

A mutual building society dedicated to improving the environment by promoting sustainable housing and sustainable communities. Savings placed with the society fund mortgage lending on: energy-efficient housing; ecological renovation; derelict and dilapidated properties; small-scale and ecological enterprise; and low-impact lifestyles.

English Heritage
Customer Services Department
PO Box 569
Swindon SN2 2YP
Tel: 0870 333 1181
www.english-heritage.org.uk

Dedicated to ensuring that the historic environment of England is properly maintained and cared for; aims to help people understand and appreciate why the historic buildings and landscapes around them matter. The details above are for general enquiries. Regional enquiries are dealt with by the offices listed below.

London Region
23 Savile Row
London W1S 2ET
Tel: 020 7973 3000

East of England Region
Brooklands House
24 Brooklands Avenue
Cambridge CB2 2BU
Tel: 01223 582700

East Midlands Region
44 Derngate
Northampton NN1 1UH
Tel: 01604 735400

Northeast Region
Bessie Surtees House
41–44 Sandhill
Newcastle upon Tyne NE1 3JF
Tel: 0191 261 1585

Northwest Region
Canada House
3 Chepstow Street
Manchester M1 5FW
Tel: 0161 242 1400
Southeast Region
Eastgate Court
195–205 High Street
Guildford GU1 3EH
Tel: 01483 252000

Southwest Region
29 Queen Square
Bristol BS1 4ND
Tel: 0117 975 0700

West Midlands Region
112 Colmore Row
Birmingham B3 3AG
Tel: 0121 625 6820

Yorkshire Region
37 Tanner Row
York YO1 6WP
Tel: 01904 601901

The Federation of Master Builders (FMB)
Gordon Fisher House
14–15 Great James Street
London WC1N 3DP
Tel: 020 7242 7583
www.fmb.org.uk

A source of knowledge, professional advice and support for its members, providing a range of modern and relevant business building services to save them time and money. The FMB is independent and non-profit-making, lobbying continuously for members' interests at both national and local levels.

Garden History Society
70 Cowcross Street
London EC1M 6EJ
Tel: 020 7608 2409
www.gardenhistorysociety.org

Promotes the study of the history of gardening, landscape gardening and horticulture; the protection and conservation of historic parks, gardens and designed landscapes, and advises on their restoration; and encourages the creation of new parks, gardens and designed landscapes

Geffrye Museum
Kingsland Road
London E2 8EA
Tel: 020 7739 9893
www.geffrye-museum.org.uk

One of London's best-loved museums. It shows the changing style of the English domestic interior in a series of period rooms from 1600 to the present day.

The Georgian Group
6 Fitzroy Square
London W1T 5DX
Tel: 020 7529 8920
www.georgiangroup.org.uk

Charity dedicated to preserving Georgian buildings and gardens.

Green Building Store
11 Huddersfield Road
Meltham
Holmfirth
West Yorkshire HD9 4NJ
Tel: 01484 854898
Fax: 01484 854899
Email:
info@greenbuildingstore.co.uk
www.greenbuildingstore.co.uk

Online shop and information source for eco-friendly building products.

Guild of Master Craftsmen
166 High Street
Lewes
East Sussex BN7 1XU
www.thegmcgroup.com

Trade association representing many different trades and professions. Brings together highly skilled people engaged in professions, vocations, crafts, arts and trades in order to safeguard the interests of craftsmen and the public.

Health and Safety Executive (HSE)
Tel: 08701 545500 (Infoline)
www.hse.gov.uk

Britain's Health and Safety Commission (HSC) and the Health and Safety Executive (HSE) are responsible for the regulation of almost all the risks to health and safety arising from work activity in Britain.

Heritage Lottery Fund
7 Holbein Place
London SW1W 8NR
Tel: 020 7591 6000
www.hlf.org.uk

Enables communities to celebrate, look after and learn more about their diverse heritage. From great museums and historic buildings to local parks and nature reserves, to recording and celebrating traditions, customs and history, HLF grants open up the nation's heritage for everyone to enjoy.

Historic Chapels Trust
29 Thurloe Street
London SW7 2LE
Tel: 020 7584 6072
www.hct.org.uk

Aims to take into ownership redundant chapels and other places of worship in England that are of outstanding architectural and historic interest. The object is to secure their preservation, repair and maintenance for public benefit, including contents, burial grounds and ancillary buildings.

Historic Gardens Foundation
34 River Court
Upper Ground
London E1 9PE
Tel: 020 7633 9165
www.historicgardens.org

A non-profit-making organization set up in 1995 to link everyone concerned with the preservation, restoration and management of historic parks and gardens.

Historic Houses Association
2 Chester Street
London SW1X 7BB
Tel: 020 7259 5688
www.hha.org.uk

Assists private owners to maintain Britain's historic houses and gardens for the benefit of the nation and for future generations.

Images of England
c/o National Monuments Record Centre
Kemble Drive
Swindon SN2 2GZ
Tel: 01793 414600
www.imagesofengland.org.uk

Funded by English Heritage and the Heritage Lottery Fund, this is a groundbreaking initiative that aims to create a 'point in time' photographic record of England's listed buildings.

Institute of Historic Building Conservation
Jubilee House
High Street
Tisbury
Wiltshire SP3 6HA
Tel: 01747 873133
www.ihbc.org.uk

Aims to establish the highest standards of conservation practice to support the effective protection and enhancement of the historic environment.

The Listed Property Owners' Club
FREEPOST
Hartlip
Sittingbourne
Kent ME9 7TE
Tel: 01795 844939
www.lpoc.co.uk

Provides tailored advice, services for owners of listed properties and the benefits of a club network.

Listing Team
see Department for Culture, Media and Sport website

Museum of Garden History
Lambeth Palace Road
London SE1 7LB
Tel: 020 7401 8865
Email: info@museumgardenhistory.org
www.museumgardenhistory.org

Exists to enhance the understanding and appreciation of the history and development of gardens and gardening in the UK. Founded in 1977 as the world's first museum dedicated to the history of gardens and gardening. Museum includes a reproduction seventeenth-century knot garden with historically accurate planting.

National Monuments Record (NMR)
National Monuments Record Centre
Great Western Village
Kemble Drive
Swindon SN2 2GZ
Tel: 01793 414600
www.english-heritage.org.uk

English Heritage's public archive – a fantastic source of information about archaeology and buildings; also has aerial photographs of England.

National Trust
36 Queen Anne's Gate
London SW1H 9AS
Tel: 0807 458 4000
www.nationaltrust.org.uk

Acts as a guardian for the nation in the acquisition and protection of threatened coastline, countryside and buildings.

Norwich and Peterborough Building Society
Peterborough Business Park (Head Office)
Lynch Wood
Peterborough PE2 6WZ
Tel: 0845 300 6727
Email: info@npbs.co.uk
www.npbs.co.uk

Provider of Special Scheme mortgages including 'brown' mortgages, designed for people who want to buy a property to convert or restore.

Office of the Deputy Prime Minister
26 Whitehall
London SW1A 2WH
Tel: 020 7944 4400
Fax: 020 7944 9622
www.odpm.gov.uk
ODPM has responsibility for local and regional government, housing, planning, fire, regeneration, social exclusion and neighbourhood renewal.

Period Property UK
www.periodproperty.co.uk

The definitive site on the web for information on period properties, their character and their maintenance.

Professional Accreditation of Conservator-Restorers (PACR)
c/o UK Institute of Conservation
109 The Chandlery
50 Westminster Bridge Road
London SE1 7QY
Tel 020 7721 8721
www.pacr.org.uk

Implements standards for the care of our cultural heritage across a range of disciplines. Conservator-restorers accredited by PACR have demonstrated to assessors that they have the appropriate knowledge, practical skills and sound professional judgement.

Regeneration Through Heritage
The Prince's Foundation
19–22 Charlotte Road
London EC2A 3SG
Tel: 020 7613 8500
www.princes-foundation.org

Teaches and demonstrates in practice those principles of traditional urban design and architecture that put people and the communities of which they are part at the centre of the design process.

Register of Architects Accredited in Building Conservation
33 Macclesfield Road
Wilmslow
Cheshire SK9 2AF
Tel: 01625 523784
www.aabc-register.co.uk

The architects listed on this register have all been assessed as to their individual knowledge and experience in conservation work by their peers in a team that also included a knowledgeable non-architect to ensure an element of public participation in the assessment process.

Royal Institute of British Architects (RIBA)
66 Portland Place
London W1B 1AD
Tel 020 7307 3700
www.riba.org

The Royal Institute of British Architects, one of the most influential architectural institutions in the world, has been promoting architecture and architects since being awarded its Royal Charter in 1837. On its useful website you can search the UK Directory of Registered Practices for an architect who specializes in restoration projects.

Royal Institution of Chartered Surveyors (RICS)
Building Conservation Group
12 Great George Street
Parliament Square
London SW1P 3AD
Tel 020 7222 7000
www.rics.org.uk

Leading source of land, property, construction and related environmental knowledge. RICS supports 110,000 members worldwide, promotes best practice, represents consumers' interests and provides impartial advice to society, businesses, governments and global organizations.

SALVO
PO Box 28080
London
SE27 0YZ
Tel: 020 8761 2316
Fax: 01890 820499
www.salvo.co.uk

The Salvo Code is a simple code for dealers who buy and sell architectural antiques and reclaimed building materials. Its aim is to give buyers confidence that items they buy have not been stolen or removed from listed or protected buildings without permission. The Salvo website offers a comprehensive listing of companies specializing in architectural salvage and includes for sale and wanted ads, dealer directories and discussion forum. Also covers reproduction pieces, restorers, eco-friendly and green building specialists.

SAVE Britain's Heritage
70 Cowcross Street
London EC1M 6EJ
Tel: 020 7253 3500
www.savebritainsheritage.org

Campaigns for threatened historic buildings.

Society for the Protection of Ancient Buildings (SPAB)
37 Spital Square
London E1 6DY
020 7377 1644
www.spab.org.uk

Largest and oldest expert national pressure group fighting to save old buildings from decay, demolition and damage.

Theatres Trust
22 Charing Cross Road
London WC2H 0HR
Tel: 020 7836 8591
www.theatrestrust.org.uk

National body whose purpose is to promote the better protection of theatres. As well as considering planning applications relating to theatre buildings, it provides help and advice on planning and design matters, campaigns on behalf of theatres, and works to foster a general interest in theatre architecture.

Traditional Paint Forum
Una Richards, Chair
c/o The National Trust for Scotland
28 Charlotte Square
Edinburgh EH2 4ET
Email: urichards@nts.org.uk

The Traditional Paint Forum (TPF) was set up in 1994 as a membership forum for discussing and promoting a better understanding and appreciation of traditional paint.

Twentieth Century Society
70 Cowcross Street
London EC1M 6EJ
Tel: 020 7250 3857
www.c20society.org.uk/index2

Specialized conservation society covering the period after 1914. Aims to foster an understanding and appreciation of the best of all kinds of buildings erected in Britain in the twentieth century.

United Kingdom Institute for Conservation of Historic and Artistic Works
702 The Chandlery
50 Westminster Bridge Road
London SE1 7QY
Tel: 020 7721 8246
www.ukic.org.uk

UKIC is the professional body representing those who care for the country's cultural objects and heritage collections. Its members are conservators working in public institutions such as museums and galleries, and conservators and restorers working in the private sector. It also aims to provide information and advice to those requiring conservation services.

Victorian Society
1 Priory Gardens
Bedford Park
London W4 1TT
Tel: 020 8993 1019
www.victorian-society.org.uk
Dedicated to the study and protection of Victorian and Edwardian architecture and other arts.

Weald & Downland Open Air Museum
Singleton
Chichester
West Sussex PO18 0EU
Tel: 01243 811348
www.wealddown.co.uk

Museum of rural life set in 50 acres of Sussex countryside. Nearly 50 historic buildings, dating from the thirteenth to the nineteenth centuries, have been rescued from destruction and restored to their original form, bringing to life the homes, farmsteads and rural industries of the last 500 years. Skilled demonstrators explain how to use traditional building techniques and conserve rural crafts.

York University Archaeology Department
Kings Manor
York YO1 7EP
Tel: 01904 433901
Email: archaeology@york.ac.uk
www.york.ac.uk/depts/arch

Offers a range of short, professional building conservation courses, including Lime Week, Church Conservation, Stone, Timber, Interiors, Plasterwork, Earth, Economics, Project Management and Risk Assessment, Brick, Modern Materials, and Metals in Architecture, provided by specialists in one of the leading centres for research and teaching in the UK.

NORTHERN IRELAND

Environment and Heritage Service
5–33 Hill Street
Belfast BT1 2LA
Tel: 028 9054 3061
www.ehsni.gov.uk

Protects and conserves Northern Ireland's natural heritage and built environment to control and regulate pollution and to promote the wider appreciation of the environment and best environmental practices. Advises and implements the government's environmental policy and strategy in Northern Ireland.

National Trust for Northern Ireland
Rowallane House
Saintfield
Ballynahinch
County Down BT24 7LH
Tel: 028 9751 0721
www.ntni.org.uk

Guardian for the nation in the acquisition and protection of threatened coastline, countryside and buildings.

Ulster Architectural Heritage Society
66 Donegall Pass
Belfast BT7 1BU
Tel: 028 9055 0313
www.uahs.co.uk

Promotes the appreciation and enjoyment of architecture from the prehistoric to the present in the nine counties of Ulster, and encourages its preservation and conservation.

SCOTLAND

Architectural Heritage Society of Scotland
Glasite Meeting House
33 Barony Street
Edinburgh EH3 6NY
Tel: 0131 557 0019
www.ahss.org.uk

Concerned with the protection, preservation, study and appreciation of Scottish buildings.

Council for Scottish Archaeology
c/o National Museums of Scotland
Chambers Street
Edinburgh EH1 1JF
Tel: 0131 247 4119
www.britarch.ac.uk/csa

Works to secure the archaeological heritage of Scotland for its people through education, promotion and support. Its key objectives are: education, both formal and informal, concerning Scotland's archaeological heritage; promotion of the conservation, management, understanding and enjoyment of, and access to, Scotland's archaeological heritage; and support through the provision of advice, guidance, resources and information relating to archaeology in Scotland.

Historic Scotland
Longmore House
Salisbury Place
Edinburgh EH9 1SH
Tel: 0131 668 8600
www.historic-scotland.gov.uk

Safeguards Scotland's built heritage and promotes its understanding and enjoyment. On their website you can find information on Scotland's listed buildings and scheduled ancient monuments. They also have details on technical conservation and research.

National Trust for Scotland
Wemyss House
28 Charlotte Square
Edinburgh EH2 4ET
Tel: 0131 243 9300
www.nts.org.uk

Protects and promotes Scotland's natural and cultural heritage for present and future generations to enjoy.

Scottish Civic Trust
The Tobacco Merchant's House
42 Miller Street
Glasgow G1 2DT
Tel: 0141 221 1466
www.scottishcivictrust.org.uk

Aims to encourage public concern for the urban and rural environment; high quality in the planning and construction of new buildings; the conservation and/or adaptation for reuse of older buildings of distinction or historic interest; informed and effective input into planning matters; the elimination of ugliness, whether resulting from social deprivation, bad design or neglect.

WALES

Cadw – Welsh Historic Monuments
Crown Buildings
Cathays Park
Cardiff CF10 3NQ
Tel: 029 2050 0200
www.cadw.wales.gov.uk

Historic environment agency within the Welsh Assembly Government, with responsibility for protecting, conserving and promoting an appreciation of the historic environment of Wales. This includes historic buildings, ancient monuments, historic parks and gardens, landscapes and underwater archaeology.

Civic Trust for Wales
3rd Floor, Empire House
Mount Stuart Square
Cardiff CF10 5FN
Tel: 029 2048 4606
www.civictrustwales.org

Promotes civic pride as a means to improving the quality of life for all in the places where we live and work, and encourages community action, good design, sustainable development and respect for the built environment among people of all ages.

Royal Commission on the Ancient and Historical Monuments of Wales
Plas Crug, Aberystwyth
Ceredigion SY23 1NJ
Tel: 01970 621200
www.rcahmw.org.uk

Surveys, records and interprets terrestrial and maritime archaeological and historical sites, structures and landscapes, particularly those of national and local importance, that are threatened with destruction.

MATERIALS

Building Limes Forum
Glasite Meeting House
33 Barony Street
Edinburgh EH3 6NX
www.buildinglimesforum.org.uk

Exists to encourage expertise and understanding in the use of building limes.

Butcher Plasterworks
Chalcot Yard
8 Fitzroy Road
London NW1 8T
Tel: 020 7722 9771
www.butcherplasterworks.com

One of the UK's few remaining specialists in traditional decorative plasterworks.

Calch Ty-Mawr Lime
Ty-Mawr Farm
Llangasty, Brecon
Powys LD3 7PJ
Tel: 01874 658249
www.lime.org.uk

Lime products, building materials, paints and finishing products, courses, projects and news, and tips, books and FAQS.

London Crown Glass Company
21 Harpsden Road
Henley on Thames
Oxfordshire RG9 1EE
Tel: 01491 413227
www.londoncrownglass.co.uk

Specializes in high-quality conservation glasses selected from the best of the traditional European craftsman glassblowers.

Picreator Enterprises Ltd
44 Park View Gardens
London NW4 2PN
Tel: 020 8202 8972
www.picreator.co.uk

Materials for professional restoration and conservation, including Renaissance Wax, Renaissance Metal De-corroder and Vulpex Liquid Soap.

Sanderson
Sanderson House
Oxford Road
Denham UB9 4DX
Tel: 01895 830044
www.sanderson-online.co.uk
Makers of William Morris & Co wallpaper and fabrics.

FURTHER READING

Ashurst, John and Nicola, *Practical Building Conservation: Vol. 1 Stone Masonry* (English Heritage 1988)
Ashurst, John and Nicola, *Practical Building Conservation: Vol. 2 Brick, Terracotta and Earth* (English Heritage 1988)
Ashurst, John and Nicola, *Practical Building Conservation: Vol. 3 Mortars, Plasters and Renders* (English Heritage 1988)
Ashurst, John and Nicola, *Practical Building Conservation: Vol. 4 Metals* (English Heritage 1988)
Ashurst, John and Nicola, *Practical Building Conservation: Vol. 5 Wood, Glass and Resin* (English Heritage 1988)
Bevan, Sally, *The Reclaimers: A Complete Guide to Salvage* (Hodder & Stoughton 2005)
de Bierre, Julia and Bain Smith, James, *Restoration Recipes* (Quadrille Publishing Ltd 1999)
Bowyer, Jack (ed), *Handbook of Building Crafts in Conservation* (Hutchinson & Co 1981)
Brereton, Christopher, *The Repair of Historic Buildings* (English Heritage 1995)
Brunskill, R.W., *Traditional Buildings of Britain* (Victor Gollancz 1992)
Brunskill, R.W., *Houses & Cottages of Britain* (Victor Gollancz 2000)
Calloway, Stephen (ed), *The Elements of Style: An Encyclopedia of Domestic Architectural Detail* (Mitchell Beazley 2004)
Collings, Janet, *Old House Care and Repair* (Donhead Publishing 2002)
Collins, John F.N., *Restoration Techniques* (Cheshire County Council County Planning Dept 1982)
Cunnington, Pamela, *Caring for Old Houses* (Marston House 2002)
Cunnington, Pamela, *How Old Is Your House?* (Marston House 2002)
Forster, Robin and Whittaker, Tim, *The Well-Worn Interior* (Thames & Hudson 2003)
Hill, P.R. and David, J.C.E., *Practical Stone Masonry* (Donhead Publishing 2000)
Holmes, Stafford and Wingate, Michael, *Building with Lime* (ITDG Publishing 2002)
Johnson, Alan, *Your Victorian House* (David & Charles 1991)
Kitchen, Judith L., *Caring for Your Old House* (John Wiley & Sons Inc 1991)
Lander, Hugh, *The House Restorer's Guide* (David & Charles 1996)
Lander, Hugh *House and Cottage Restoration* (Acanthus Books 1999)
McAfee, Patrick, *Stone Buildings: Conservation, Repair, Building* (The O'Brien Press Ltd 1998)
Miller, Judith, *Period Details Sourcebook* (Mitchell Beazley 2003)
Miller, Judith, *The Style Sourcebook* (Mitchell Beazley 2003)
Miller, Judith and Martin, *Period Finishes and Effects* (Mitchell Beazley 1992)
Morris, Alistair, *Antiques from the Garden* (Garden Art Press 2001)
O'Gorman, Thomas J., *New Spaces from Salvage* (PRC Publishing 2002)
Owen, Jane and Gavin, Diarmuid, *Gardens Through Time* (BBC Books 2004)
Parissien, Steven, *The Georgian House* (Aurum Press Ltd 1999)
Pearson, David, *The Natural House Book* (Conran Octopus Ltd 1995)
Roberts, Alan, *Architectural Antiques* (Unwin Hyman 1987)
Spencer-Churchill, Henrietta, *Classic Interior Design* (Cico Books 2003)
Taylor, Patrick, *Period Gardens* (Pavilion Books Ltd 1996)
Thornton, Peter, *Authentic Décor: The Domestic Interior 1620–1920 (Cassell and Co 2000)*
Weaver, Martin, *Conserving Buildings* (John Wiley & Sons Inc 1997)
Van Der Werff, Rupert and Rees, Jackie, *Miller's Guide to Garden Antiques* (Octopus Publishing Ltd 2003)

INDEX

PICTURE CREDITS

BBC Worldwide would like to thank the following for providing photographs and permission to reproduce copyright material. While every effort has been made to trace and acknowledge all copyright holders, we would like to apologize should there have been any errors or omissions.

BBC Homes & Antiques Magazine 29 (*below right*), 51 (*below right*), 57, 66, 67, 78, 89, 95, 96, 103, 109 (*left*), 131, 133, 148-151, 174-176, 185 (*right*), 196, 197, 204, 205, 207 (*right*), 208, 216-219,223;

BBC Worldwide Ltd/Robin Matthews 1,7;

Collections 22, 24, 25, 32-34, 47, 49, 51 (*above left*), 56, 60-62, 64, 65, 82, 91, 93, 98 (*right*), 99, 102, 105, 109 (*right*), 111-113, 123-125, 129, 130, 135-137, 141, 153, 159, 170 (*left*), 179-181, 185 (*left*), 193, 203, 209, 227, 233, 237, 240;

Edifice 16-21, 23 (*right*), 27, 29 (*below left*), 31, 36, 41, 63, 69, 75-77, 87, 88 (*right*), 90, 104, 108, 121, 133 (*below right*), 138, 140, 147, 155, 157, 164, 166, 169, 170 (*right*), 171, 172, 185 (*center*), 195, 220-222, 224, 242;

Corporation of London / Heritage-Images 122;

Maya Vision International Ltd 101;

Narratives/J. Baldwin/P. Eltes 189, 191 (*left*);

National Trust Photographic 23 (*left*), 29 (*above left*), (*above right*), 45, 51 (*above right*), (*below left*), 55, 71, 79-81, 83-85, 97, 98l, 100, 107, 119, 126, 152, 154, 160, 165, 168, 173, 177, 182-184, 187, 190, 191 (*right*), 192, 194, 199, 202, 206, 207 (*left*), 211-214, 225, 228-232, 234-236, 238, 239, 241, 243;

Shakespeare Birthplace Trust 201;

Weald & Downland Open Air Museum 74.

All other images by the *Restored to Glory* production team: photographers Clare Bradbury, Julia Jarvis, Mike Maclaine, Caroline Matthews.